MARY'S
MESSAGE
OF
LOVE

ALLAN ARTHUR SCHULTE

PUBLISHED BY
THE MARY FOUNDATION
SARASOTA, FLORIDA

Mary's
Message
of
Love

Library of Congress Control Number: 2001091168
ISBN 0970492405

Internet: http://www.MarysMessage.com
Fax: 941-923-6331

If you are unable to order this book from your local bookseller,
you may order it directly.
Quantity discounts for organizations are available.
Contact:
Light Education, Inc.
P.O. Box 15043
Sarasota, Florida 34277

Printed in the United States of America

For

Marcia Wright Schulte

who taught me the value of listening to my heart,

and who has been far more than a wife to me...

best friend, partner and a seeker of truth.

For

Brooke and Evan Schulte,

my daughters,

who both allowed room for love...

so that miracles could blossom

all around us.

Contents

PART THREE – TAKING THE TIME TO PRAY

PART FOUR – CHALLENGES OF NURTURING

PART FIVE – CAUGHT BETWEEN FEAR & LOVE

PART SIX – ON SEX & SEXUALITY

PART SEVEN - MONEY & SUPPORT IN LIFE

PART EIGHT - VICTIMS, NEW AGE & DRUGS

PART NINE - SACREDNESS

Part Ten - Being a Big Person

Part Eleven - Living Your Life With Spiritual Intelligence

Part Twelve - My Mary Mission

Acknowledgments

I wish to thank the hundreds of people who have been part of the process of this book.

First of all, I wish to thank Mary for her faithfulness to us all, along with her clarity and her strong direction in giving us this book. The presence of her love was a warm, honest and deep experience.

Next I would like to thank my immediate family, my wife, Marcia, who encouraged me to stand firm in Mary's voice and her message, who helped me edit the book and prepare it for printing. She has been a loving and guiding Light and I am deeply grateful for her love. I would like to thank my wonderful daughters, Brooke and Evan, who loved Mary's words and constantly encouraged the book.

Sincere gratitude to Donna Sweeney of Boston who read the text and decided that this message was meant for the benefit of the world, "Let's get this into print and into people's hands!" Many thanks to Donna for her Light and her encouragement of this project. I am happy that she is our publishing partner.

A very big thank you to Dorothy Spelman, our dear Miracles friend, whose loving editing of the final text was so very appreciated. Special thanks to our friends Ed and Chorale Page who encouraged this work, and to Rean Wegley and Pat Martin for their insights. Thanks to Nancy Myers for providing a quiet space for the project to grow. Special thanks to all our Course in Miracles friends who helped in the process, especially Gordon Swenson, Phil Snider, Jay Whitham, Wendy Nethersole and Bobbie Benz for their encouragement— along with Ginger Daniel, Bishop Mark Libowitz of the Madonna Ministry and Nancy O'Connor.

Special thanks to Sara Jane Freymann, our literary agent in New York, who saw the book early on and loved its strength and authenticity. Mary's words spoke to her and she made it known. Thanks to the editors at Doubleday, Broadway/Bantam/Dell, Random House, Viking-Penguin and Ballantine for their encouragement of the book. Thanks to Layne Moore and his staff who were so helpful with the printing. To Judy Webster who did the text layout and created the beautiful cover.

Thanks to all my many teachers from the Jesuits to my professors at Notre Dame. Thanks to Father Theodore Hesburgh, C.S.C., former president of the University of Notre Dame, for his kind words regarding the early portion of this message, and to Father Edward O'Connor, Notre Dame's Marian Scholar Emeritus, for his suggestions in the process. Thanks to Bishop Charles Sommers of California who encouraged and ordained me as a Madonna Minister in the service of Mary. And to the Reverend Joseph Clifford from Incarnation Catholic Church for his reading of the original text and his encouragement of the book. Thanks to my many spiritual teachers including the Reverend David Johnson, Bill Moore, the Reverend Hunter Isaacs, and Mary Osborne, as well as Marianne Williamson, Arnold Patent, Joel Goldsmith, Ken Wapnick and Jon Mundy, who have also been such helpful teachers. Most of all, thank you, Holy Spirit, for your consistent encouragement and leadership in this project. (We could have done nothing without You!)

Thanks to my mother, Ruth Anne, for introducing me to Mary when I was still in my crib, and for the spiritual discipline and reverence she imparted to our family.

Thanks to my late father, Allan, and my mother for their encouragement and enthusiam for life, along with their support of a Notre Dame education. Thanks to my brothers, Tom and William, and my sister, Marianne, for their enduring friendship. Special thanks to all my friends in our Course in Miracles group, and for all the love, light and support I experience constantly in my life.

Allan Schulte
February 2001

Allan Schulte, with whom Mary shared her Message of Love, and his wife, Marcia, felt it would be helpful to readers to share about the background of this book.

Preface

About the Background of this Book

I would like to share with you briefly how Mary began this work. It happened very simply. It was during the Christmas holidays that Mary announced the project, saying: "Get ready, Allan. We're going to start a writing project when the holidays are over." I recognized her voice because I've known her presence for some time.

Mary's regular messages began on the day after New Year's. I was up early that morning and had just finished making coffee when I heard the words, "This is the day. It's time for us to start." I got my writing pad, sat down, and Mary started in on her dictation. Her words were very simple and direct.

This was the start of a long and consistent dictation. It was a pleasant way to begin the day. Each morning Mary would dictate for about an hour and then say, "We are complete for today."

I would say, "I can go on, Mary. I'm not tired." "No," she would say, "that is enough. We are complete for today. We will begin again tomorrow." And so her writings grew, day by day. We worked together for six weeks on her book. She was very clear about the conclusion of the project. "It is complete. That is all for now." She was always very definitive. There was nothing vague about her direction.

A couple of weeks into the project I thought it might be easier to work at the computer because I am a fairly quick typist. But Mary felt that typing on a keyboard was not an improvement. She preferred that I take her words down on paper longhand. The typing process was too fast. In order to hear her words accurately, evenly, at the right speed, the slower process of handwriting, she said, was desirable. It was true.

When these messages began to come through from Mary, it was with an ease and simplicity. I was not searching for them at that time.

The process of working with Mary has been easy because I have known Mary as a spiritual mother and friend most of my life. Our friendship started when I was a boy, continued when I was an altar boy, and later through the sodality at my Jesuit school. But it grew particularly strong during my under-graduate years at Notre Dame. There, Mary's presence was everywhere, but particularly at the Grotto, a replica of the shrine at Lourdes. The Grotto had a very strong sense of Mary's presence which has remained with me throughout my life. It has helped me to stay close to Mary – and to feel very comfortable with her.

Many times during the period this work was being dictated, I would ask if it were true that this was Mary's spirit, her soul talking actively with such sureness, such strength. And always there was confirmation, always the same quiet, inner assurance to trust in her, to work with her. Her Inner Light would always reconfirm this for me. And I would hear reassurance from the Holy Spirit at the same time. His reassurance would always come in the form of a rich, full vibration in both ears – like a vibration of both eardrums, simultane-ously. It sounded like wind – like a strong wind through the trees. It was a very full sound. It still happens whenever I ask for confirmation, as right now, when I am writing this.

Mary's presence felt more like a soft mantle that was being placed on my shoulders. Her thanks would come often, saying thank you for bringing this material forward. She often reminded me that many of her children in the world could be very cynical. Mary said many times that it was hard for her messages to be accepted with assurance on earth. She kept asking for a way for her voice to be heard in the world. She would say again and again that she could not be heard without people like me, and would I, please, just trust her.

Working with Mary has been a joy and a pleasure. I found her to be both powerful and comforting. I felt she had a very strong will and purpose. Yet, she had a beautiful gentleness about her.

Mary said that her purpose in creating more of a presence here on earth is to be a light-bearer for us. It is her mission to assist her Son, Jesus Christ, in whatever way He asks. He has asked her specifically to help teach forgiveness, to reawaken souls that are half-asleep in life, to open hearts. She has come to share the process of the "Undoing" and to be a catalyst for love.

Mary made it clear that she was not here just to help Catholics. "I am here for the people of the world. Their religion is not important to me. I am here to help all of my Children who need my nurturing."

Mary said that she was writing for two reasons: to share some basic Truths with her Children about the spiritual path and to have a voice in today's world.

Mary feels that the noise of the world keeps us all very preoccupied. The media and the illusionary world that television creates, along with all the TV chatter, the music, electronics and the constant busy-ness of contemporary life — these distractions have made it more difficult for her, for Christ, for the Holy Spirit, to do their work of healing from within.

This is one of the reasons that Mary has expressed her need for a stronger voice in the world.

Mary would like you to feel her inner light when you read her words. The real point of the book, as she states it, is to give you a message of love to res-onate within your heart, to help you open your heart even wider to love's pres-ence, which ultimately means to the flow of God's energy through your heart.

I thank Mary for trusting me with her words. I have listened carefully and conscientiously in an effort to be a clear channel and to put everything down accurately, in the spirit of her truth and light. Mary has not been a taskmaster. I found her to be very gentle – similar to the Holy Spirit. She was there to bring clarity and light to our journey.

I am happy to have been able to help in this process. Taking down her words has been a joyful experience. I am happy for all of the people it will help. I hope that you will feel her grace and her protection expanding contin-ually, as you read this book. I hope you, too, will come to enjoy her happiness, and be warmed by her light and her love.

Allan Schulte
January 2001

Introduction

Comments on the
Writing of this Book

By Marcia Wright Schule

FROM OUR FIRST MEETING IN 1970, I HAVE COME TO KNOW ALLAN very intimately as husband, partner and friend. The most amazing realization to me was that this tall, handsome man really loved God.

My spiritual life has always been very important to me. But until I met him, I doubted I would ever find a man I was interested in who would have a deep spiritual nature.

Allan and I have been in love now for over 30 years; we have been married for 29 of those years. In truth, the Virgin Mary was one of the few touchy subjects in our marriage.

Shortly after we met, Allan mentioned to me that he had a great devotion to Mary that started when he was very young. This closeness to her continued when he was a young boy, building altars to Mary in the woods. It continued during his years as an altar boy, while a student at a Jesuit high school, and on through his college years at Notre Dame. There, he liked attending mass in the many chapels on campus and especially lighting candles at Our Lady's Grotto.

I ignored his relationship with Mary. Occasionally I would find a rosary or a holy card with Mary's picture on it lying among his things. My reaction was – ah well, he still believes in Santa Claus!

Having been brought up a Presbyterian, we recognized Mary as the mother of Jesus in a historical sense. We appreciated her motherly qualities of love and forbearance — but she certainly wasn't up there with the Trinity. She had her place at Christmas, but she was not a focal point in our Protestant world.

I had studied many Madonnas in my time because I was an art history major. I traveled through Europe and visited the important churches and museums that had major paintings and sculptures of Mary by Giotto, Botticelli, Leonardo da Vinci, and Michelangelo. Seldom was I emotionally moved by the subject matter. I did not catch the passion, the mystical quality that these works of art were supposed to evoke.

Through most of our marriage, spiritual growth has been a major part of our lives. Our spiritual "questing" has been continuous. Allan has continually brought home new books. We would read and discuss these books daily. Our conversations were always filled with this passionate pursuit of truth.

Our life has been filled with the big questions: What's the purpose of life? What does God want us to do? We taught Christian education. We attended spiritual-growth seminars. We interacted with hundreds of people on these topics. Bookshelves in nearly every room of our house overflow with spiritual books. And people flow through our home and our lives – other souls also in quest of the answers. We spent much time processing, interacting and learning through seminars and classes.

Allan is a natural student and teacher. He delves, he studies, and he discusses. Through all the uncertainties of his life, Allan has always stayed true to his faith. He has been a teacher to me and to many others, mostly by how he lives his life. He and I have been Course in Miracles teachers for a decade, leading book discussions and spiritual study groups. There has been an obvious transformation in so many lives – choosing love, living forgiveness. The *undoing* of the ego process really works.

I noticed in January that Allan was getting up earlier and earlier each morning. We really don't keep secrets from each other, but he seemed to hesitate when I asked him one evening what was happening. "I'm writing," he answered.

"Great," I said. "What?" "It's a kind of automatic writing. I'm receiving messages," he replied. "Oh," I asked, "From whom?" "From Mary, the Blessed Mother. She says she wants a voice in the world."

I was silent. Mary? She's back, I thought… Maybe these childlike notions never left him….

Then a calmness, a deep peace settled over me. It's natural, I thought. If a soul is continuous, then why can't Mary's soul still be awake and alive? If many other souls are communicating through channels, why not Mary?

I felt a real joy for Allan. In a way I could see that he had been preparing for this all his life. He has been so true to his faith, his love of God, his Christness, and his relationship with Mary. After a month of writing, Allan asked me to look over the manuscript. Tears came to my eyes. There was Truth here. This is an active woman with a mission, a "contemporary" woman who truly desires to help her children – all God's children.

This is one project we have not shared. My input has been very limited – to editing and organization of the material. But Allan and I have been so close all these years that I am very aware of his writing style, his expressions and vocabulary. Although most of this book agrees with his belief system, not all of it does. Also, this is not his style or method of writing. Allan will often write and rewrite until his writing is concise. I have helped him edit many scripts and business proposals. Never have I seen his own writing appear so concise with the first draft. This book has a different energy, clarity and lightness.

Allan is a very fast typist and he seldom writes longhand. I was truly surprised when I found him writing longhand on yellow legal pads and not using his computer.

The Mary personality comes through as quite different from Allan's own. While Allan has a loving nature and cares about people, this Presence has a deep compassion for children and is extremely focused as to what is wrong in the world and how to change it.

This voice has been a mother, a nurturer, and an encourager of children. Although Allan has been a wonderful, involved parent, his role has been much different – the peacemaker, the spiritual head of our home, the disciplinarian, the conciliator. My role in our family has been more the encourager, the consistent nurturer, the listener.

At this time I have not had any personal communications from Mary except through Allan. And I have to admit I'm a bit embarrassed by my previous, limited viewpoint of her. But she comes through as so loving and desirous of helping us; I can't help but want to hear her, too.

For now I am content to be a reader. The concept of Mary's speaking to us today is still quite foreign to me, but I'm getting used to Allan's relationship with her.

I feel Mary's message transcends religious differences and is a call to all of God's children to come together in love and forgiveness.

Marcia Wright Schulte
March 2001

Part One

Mary's Message

MARY'S PREFACE

MY CHILDREN, I AM SENDING THESE WORDS TO ALL OF YOU ON earth with great purpose.

I want to become part of the fabric of your world society as a contemporary Blessed Mother of today. I want to have an active voice in today's world. I want my words to be published and read. I want my work to be available to people across the world in many languages.

It is important to listen to me, because my presence is needed in your world today. There is much hurt in the world, many problems, much loneliness and depression. Many of my Children feel lost. My help is needed now, and I have a major role to play in the healing process of the world. Many of my Children are advancing toward Grace, but very slowly. Sometimes, there is more regression than progress. That is why I am here to help.

I am here to share Truths of Love, of Understanding, of Forgiveness. I am here to re-state Jesus Christ's words in a fresh way – in a way that people will understand today. And I am here to bring Grace. This is all to your mutual benefit. I am here to be who I truly am, a Soul who is still living and interacting today.

Just as my Son came back to earth after His death to finish His work among His apostles, so I come back to you to finish my work as your spiritual teacher and mother. As you say in your world: *A mother's work is never done.* And I can say the same – my work is not *nearly* done. I am here to deliver a relevant message with clarity. And I will do it in a number of ways – until all of you understand my message of Love.

My language will come out in the style that you use today. I want it to be comfortable for you to read and understand. My communication is the language of Love. I am a voice for Truth – ultimate Truth and Love.

Each of you is capable of hearing me and knowing me intimately. Some of you already hear me often and acknowledge my presence. Have the confidence and self-esteem to know that I can be with you whenever you call on me. I always have the time to come to you. My presence is open to you. I have the gift of "all-presence," and can be in an infinite number of places simultaneously.

You will know you are hearing me because you will feel an intensification of Peace, an inner thrill, that will leave you with a feeling of Joy. It is a very quiet thing. With some of you it may happen many times a day. Be open to it.

Remember that my Love for you is unconditional. And so I wish to tell you how much I love you all as perfect Children of God. In my role as your spiritual mother, I am here to nurture you and to help you through Grace. This is an all-important part of my relationship with each of you – to share Grace with you.

Some of you will not like the Truths I am sharing with you because they do not agree with what you have placed in your mind at the present. They may not agree with the way you were brought up to understand certain principles, through your own inferences, or from teachings you received. Some of you may feel anger about this. Some of you may feel violent about it. If either of those feelings comes up for you, it is all the more sure that parts of you need healing. I ask you to love yourself in such moments.

Come to me for the Grace to see things in a new Light. I am here to bring you new Light. Come to me for that enlightenment.

As you grow in your understanding of the Truth, you will come to understand the principles I am sharing with you. You will accept this with Love, and will not be judgmental. Whenever you are judgmental it is because you are feeling guilt. Let it go. One hundred times, let it go. The principles of my message will teach you to choose Love instead of fear. Whenever you disagree with the Love message I am sending you it will be because of fear. And all fear can be healed.

I have two other points I would like to share with you:

First, I wish to thank all of my many Children across the world who have been part of the *people helping people* movement. I am happy and pleased with all of your progress and accomplishments. You are making the world a gentler place for your brothers and sisters to live in.

By this I am referring to *people helping people* through charities, churches, foundations and welfare agencies, through non-profits and grass roots projects. I see all the wonderful work that is being done and for this I have deep gratitude in my heart. There has been enormous progress in this area throughout the world. I am proud of you and you should be proud of yourselves for all you have accomplished.

But there still are millions of Souls passing through the earth who are not touched by the *people helping people* movement. There are so many lost Souls who do not see a point to life. They wander aimlessly through their days, half-asleep, wondering what life is about, waiting for death to deliver them. I am here to tell you that there is no delivery in death. Death is just a continuity of consciousness on another level. Death solves nothing. I am here to give you a wake-up call. You can achieve Heaven now. Whatever consciousness you create in life, you take with you onto the next level. There is no copping out.

Second, I am not happy about the way I am perceived in today's world. I prefer not to be thought of as a Madonna or as a saint from long ago. I do not want to be thought of as a statue with a halo on an altar. You may still see me that way if you wish. But if you keep me hostage to the past, then it is like keeping me as a calcified image. I am so much more than a historical person.

I am asking you to revise the way you see me. I am not a historical virgin. I am a contemporary leader. I am always contemporary because I live in the *Now Moment*. Please see me that way.

In Truth, I am alive and very relevant to life and love today. In Truth, I am a Soul with a great mission. And I am still very active throughout the universe. I am a spiritual Soul living in the Now Moment. I am creating a voice in today's world because I have much to share of Love and Grace. And I do want my Children to listen to my words.

I want my Children to update the way they see me. I want to be re-evaluated, to be seen as a Mary who is very relevant to today's world. I want to be seen as a living force for Love in the world. I want to be seen through the eyes of Love.

Those who have seen me only as a passive virgin have not seen me in my fullness. I have a passion to care for my Children. I have a passion for the joining of all Souls as One in Heaven, One with our Father.

I am here to help all of you wake up and become relevant — now, right here in this world. To do this, I need more than sweet, comforting prayers. I need prayers of action. I need decisions for Love.

To those of you who invite me and welcome me – and I already interact with many of you – I am sharing comfort and Grace, as an Inner Comforter. But in recent years I have become very transparent to many of you in the world. Some of you often look right past me, not realizing that I am close by, bringing you comfort and Grace.

Too few of you call upon me for help in the world. I can help you with everyday problems. I am here for your spiritual support. And so I must remind you — life is a spiritual journey; it is much more than mere physical existence on the world's plane. So please do not underestimate the many ways I can bring help on your behalf. Call on me for help in everything.

It makes me sad that so many of my Children wander around the earth, half-asleep. It is as if many of you are in a waking dream. Many of you *are* in that state. And many more of you are not sure why you are on earth, or what you are supposed to be doing with your lives. I know that some of you are open to answers – especially those of you who are sad, depressed and missing the point of life. I am here to show you the way to happiness and Love.

I also know that many of my Children are cynical. I realize that you do this to protect yourself because you have been disillusioned before in your life. But to my cynical Children, I must remind you that just because you have been hurt should not mean that you close the door to acceptance, trust and under-standing. How else are we to reach you if you become worldlywise, tough and a know-it-all? My cynical Children do not know it all. They merely think they know how to protect and insulate themselves on the worldly level. My cynical Children will have to learn how to open their hearts to Love and Grace in order to make progress in this lifetime. I am here to help you do that.

Remember always that I am a Mother of Love. I am not coming here to warn you against any dangers. I am here to embrace you and to remind you that you have nothing to fear. Fear would be against everything I am. I have come to spread my Love through these writings. I am here to tell you that you have a wonderful future.

I have chosen Allan to be my channel because he has strong communica-tion abilities and he has the right mindset to handle my work. Some of you may wonder why I have not chosen a child, as I have many times in the past. Their mindset, too, is pure and strong and free from doubt. But my current message is too complex for a child to deliver.

Others may wonder why I have chosen a man, rather than a woman, to channel this message. In the past I have chosen many women to deliver my messages, but this time I have chosen a male. I always choose the right person for the message, and this has nothing to do with gender. In the new era into which you are all moving, gender will not be as much of an issue as it has been in the past. You will in time learn to forgive the subtle prejudice you have against one another, based on gender. As you continue to evolve, men will have the same abilities as women to be soft, gentle, loving, strong, understanding, expressive and whole in themselves.

It is important for each of you to continue to be free of sexist views, and to practice this in your daily life. Each Soul has a male and a female side. Each of you is a perfect Child of God. God made you in His image. Honor the wholeness of that thought because it is your reality. In Allan I have chosen a Soul who is balanced and integrated. He is the most integrated Soul I could find who has all the diverse talents I need for my mission. He already lives many of the principles in my book, and he listens.

Read my message and absorb it. This book is the beginning of my new communication with you. Try to live some of these ideas, even if they are a stretch for you. I am with you now and always in Peace, in Truth, in Grace and Love. Reach out to me.

Mary

Love with a Capital L

Please note that in most instances throughout this book the word Love will be spelled with a Capital L. This was Mary's wish because Love refers to God and His Divine energy flow. She considers the word Love synonymous with God Himself. Other words such as Children, Light, Grace, Soul, Joy and Truth also are capitalized because she considers them to be in direct relationship to and a direct extension of God.

The Opening Of Your Heart

My Children, I come to you through the form of this book to help you open your hearts. I would like to assure you of five things:

First, I am here to remind you of your purpose in life. And that is to live life actively, and to live it in Love, in a spirit of outreach. It saddens me to see so many of you living illusionary lives in front of your television sets, your games and your computers. It is your opportunity and privilege here on earth to interact with others – to have experiences – to open your hearts to one another – to live with joy – to know happiness. We will go into each of these points in more detail later in my message. Be assured I am here to help you wake up.

Second, I am here to assure you that God is Love. This is an enormously important message. As many of your churches already teach – God is All-Loving, He is Goodness, He is Light, He is Perfection.

And thus He is not a God of punishment. He is not a God of revenge. He is not a God "out to get you." He cannot be Love and be mean at the same time. That is a contradictory idea. The old ideas about God being a punishing God are from the Old Testament. They were primitive and fearful ideas about God.

They were born in guilt. Those ideas have no basis in Love. It is time to dissolve those ideas from your thought process. The time has come to fully see God through the eyes of Love. It is time for you to become acquainted with this True God who is unconditionally Loving. We will go into this in more depth later on.

Third, I am here so that you will see me, Mary, through the eyes of today. Please do not think of me as a historical person. Please do not think of my Son, Jesus Christ, that way, either. The past is over. It has no value except for the Love that was there. The only place that God or Christ or the Holy Spirit lives is in the Now. In the Present Moment. So do not look for us in the past, for you will find only a tired memory. We are alive and vital and active Souls. We interact constantly in the Present Moment on earth. This is a new awareness that each of you must nurture and grow. The Holy Spirit, your Inner Teacher, is also with you each moment to help you with each decision as you live your life.

Fourth, I am here to help you with your evolution of life. In your life here on earth, most of you are evolving. There has been much Soul progress on earth, whether you can see it or not. Many new lessons are being learned constantly. But each of you needs to keep moving forward, with progress, with Love. That is why I have come. There are new ways of seeing that will help you. And that is my fourth mission right now – your spiritual evolution. Helping you to see your life as a journey with meaning.

And fifth, I am here to give you insights on issues in today's world. Whether you are tired, confused, or despondent because of the complex world in which you live, I am here to share some Light on everyday topics that may help you on the journey.

Anyone who dislikes my new message – because it does not agree with your old images of the past – you are missing my message. Life is about seeing the old things in new ways. The message is that I am here in the now, that Christ and the Holy Spirit are here in the now, and the only thing that ultimately matters is *Love* in the *Now*.

I know that change is difficult for some of you. Truly, it is much harder for some of my Children than others. And I realize that change is absolutely terrifying to some of you. But without changes in your old ways of perceiving life, you will stay stuck at the level where you are now. I do not advocate complacency in this area. It is acceptable to be complacent about your car, your job, your home. These things do not matter in the wide scheme of your life. But it is not acceptable to be complacent about your old, conventional ways of seeing yourself and seeing life.

I am here to wake you up to everything that you are, so that you can see yourself through the eyes of Grace.

I know that many of you have an investment in the old ways of seeing things, and that you may feel threatened by adopting new ideas as part of your thinking. It may mean that you may lose some ground in the world, or that you may lose certain controls you have over parts of your worldly life. That is the price you must pay for growth. With the change you will gain more freedom and happiness; a bigger, more exciting life will open up for you. And I will be there to remind you: "I told you so! See how wonderful life can become."

As your Mother I am an encourager. I will champion you each step of the way through your evolvement. And you can count on me for my faithfulness and my loyalty.

This change is not about loss of control – it is about the very flow of life. The freedom of using your free will to live life fully.

We respect the libraries, the thought patterns and the traditions of the past. It is beautiful to have repositories of history. And we can admire the beauty of the past. But the real lessons you are here to learn are learned in everyday life. They are daily lessons about forgiveness and Love. They can only be learned in the Now Moment. So try not to become lost or sidetracked by the past. To do so is only an excuse not to pay attention to the current Truth. As your Mother I will be firm about this.

This new book I am giving you is *not* about intellectual religious positioning. And it is not about religion or the letter of the law. My message is about the spirit of Love. That is what my Son, Jesus, came to teach you. That is what God is. That is the issue and the focus at hand. I have been asked to come down to help you accelerate your progress. My current mission is extremely purposeful.

ABOUT MY NEW MISSION

Being able to communicate clearly and freely with you, my Children, has not been an easy task. Finding someone who could hear me accurately and clearly, and also have the courage to get my word out and published, has been a challenge. That person also had to believe in me, as well as in himself — clearly and with integrity. So through this communication channel we finally have such a vehicle. The import of my message has much to do with timeliness. In the past, I sometimes spoke briefly, through young Children. But at this point in time my message needs to be more specific and more detailed so that I can help you in a way that will effect the *celestial speedup* necessary to the Father's purpose and the request of my Son. Unless you are all clearer on the intent and purpose of your life, you and your children may have to repeat the life cycle endlessly. That is the major purpose of this outreach message to you.

Regarding authenticity, I am certain that some of you will question whether this message actually came from me, Mary, your Spiritual Mother. So, I will remind you of this Truth: Each of you has been blessed with the gift of *Free Will* and *Inner Truth*. Do my words resonate with the Truth in you? If so, follow your Truth within. I will impart Grace to each of you who are open to it, to learn how to live through Love. This is opposed to learning through fear. I will show you how to live by Grace rather than suffering. This will take openness and honesty on your part.

The authenticity of what I am saying to you will come from your own heart. And you will come to know my authenticity because of the progress you will see in your life as you work along with me and follow my suggestions. That will be the authenticity that will benefit you. It will come from you, from within.

If you wish to be cynical and to learn through fear, you will stay in a holding pattern. I cannot help you until you are ready to open your heart. Eventually through the stress of life – or a future life – you will break down your tough outer shell and be ready to learn. Be assured I will be there for you. So the question of authenticity is up to you, not to me. I am not here to prove myself to you. We are all One. I stand for Truth and Beauty and Light and Love. There is only One Truth and One Beauty and One Light and One Love. I am inviting you to join me, to experience this inner Lightness of being.

Some of you may be lost and have no interest in coming into the Light. In that case, I can do nothing for you until you are ready. But if you have my book – even if it sits on a shelf until the day you are ready – the day you are in crisis – that is when you may be ready to open up your heart. This book will be there, waiting for you. Its message of Love and Truth will be there to comfort you and to help bring you closer to the Light. Put this book onto the shelf of lost friends and lost family members, so it will be there when they need it. I am always ready to nurture that Soul when it is ready.

Please know that you will be deeply blessed for making my thoughts available to others who may be lost. You are all bearers of the Light. I love you, my Children, and I will not leave you, as you need help now, moving into and adjusting to the new millennium. All my Children are special and gifted. All have the gift of hearing my word. Not all of you are willing to accept that gift, however. May this message help you to realize the important role that forgiveness will play in the acceptance of your own innocence and perfection.

I ask my Children not to be critical of my message, not to pick it apart and be judgmental. If you are cynical toward my words, you will be missing the point entirely. I am asking you to learn to open your heart and not to judge. This is an important step for many of you. I ask you to accept my words with an open heart and to understand the spirit in which my message is given to you.

While my message may seem new to you, it is an ancient message and one that my Son gave nearly 2,000 years ago when He walked in your world. The message has not changed. Nor has its honesty and simplicity. Realize that everyone may not be ready to hear my message, and that is perfectly under-standable. To those I say wait – the time will come when your ears are ready. But do not wait forever. You are here on earth to make progress. This message is a wake-up call.

CHILDREN OF GOD — STOP FEARING YOUR FATHER

My Children, what did we do to deserve this dream called life on earth? We human souls took ourselves seriously eons ago when we wanted to be like God Himself. We all should have laughed at this silliness. We were already One. We were already part of God. But we took ourselves and our silly, small idea of separation from God seriously and we forgot to laugh at our ridicu-lousness. We couldn't become God or compete with God. *We already were one with God.* That was our little human error that turned out to be a large error.

Of course, we could have reversed our thought in an instant. But we for-got to laugh. We took ourselves seriously. And many of us have taken ourselves too seriously ever since. And so, out of fear and guilt, we separated ourselves from the consciousness of God the Father. Of course, this is a temporary situ-ation because He is still waiting for our return. But the problem is that many of our human brothers and sisters have taken themselves and this separation seriously. And they have been in hiding from God ever since.

But now it is time to wake up and stop this ancient fear. I tell you, laugh-ter is very close to Godliness. Laughter is an important part of your Divine her-itage. Laughter and Love will get you out of this predicament called the world.

What my Children may not realize and remember is that God is all about Love. That is All He Is. He is Perfection and Truth and Light. When you can accept this – when you can hold this Truth about God in your consciousness – then that is the God that will be reflected back to you. And then you will be back in Heaven, no matter where you are.

Whatever image you hold about God in your heart is the image that will guide your life. When your image of God is truly Loving and Beautiful, then that is the kind of life you will lead.

The Truth is that many, many human Souls are still very fearful of God. They are very afraid that God the Father is going to punish them when they meet Him face to face at death, or later at the Last Judgment. Please forget the idea of a final judgment, per se, my Children. It will not be a "judgment" because Love does not judge. Rather, call it the Second Coming. This will be a great moment when all Souls are joined in union once again with the Christ Light. The Second Coming is our coming back to God. There is nothing to worry about. We are not involved in a process of judgment, but a process of joining.

God is perfect Love. He does not know – He does not even hold in His consciousness – anything about the realm of error or guilt. It is foreign to a consciousness of Perfect Love. Of course, punishment is unknown to Him. So please – RELAX. God is not your enemy. Allow me to share with you that God the Father is such total, flawless, gorgeous, all-encompassing Love — that even to notch a couple of planes closer to The Presence is a stupendous experience. It is so wonderful to be in The Presence that once you gain this level of Grace you no longer even RETAIN the memory of sin, guilt, or fear. Those limitations would only negate Who and What He Is. I ask theologians not to quibble intellectually about what God is, or isn't, to reduce His significance. You owe your Father awe and reverence.

Because you are Children of God, you cannot languish here on earth forever. You are part of the whole, and you must eventually go back to being part of God again. To do this, you must separate yourself from this error/dream called the world, and you must leave behind the guilt, the fear, the pain, the sickness, the suffering – all the mad ideas you have made up about what constitutes life on earth.

The Truth that I am advocating DOES work! Many of you have already distanced yourself from the old ways of looking at the world. Some people are highly evolved in the Undoing and the way in which they see the world. I assure you that there are many people who truly live "Heaven on Earth."

God sent the Holy Spirit to help us in this "vale of tears," so to speak. This Comforter dwells within each of us to help us with our personal Undoing, our spiritual path back to God. The Undoing is like the peeling of an onion, layer by layer.

In this process, the Holy Spirit is your personal Inner Guide. He is your link to the Divine. He is very gentle, very loving. But in order to hear His voice, you have to be quiet. He will always speak to you in the gentlest way. He respects your free will. And He is always there when you need Him. He is never pushy.

Both Jesus Christ and I work in conjunction with Him. We are always there for you – as are your angels. So you are never really alone or abandoned.

I AM THE BLESSED MOTHER, THE MOTHER OF JESUS

I am Mary, the Blessed Mother. Some of my Children call me the Blessed Virgin. I am the mother of Jesus Christ. I am the same Mary that you may remember: from Banneux, Lourdes, Guadeloupe, La Salette, Fatima, or Mejugorge. Wherever I appeared it was always my same Soul presence of Mary. You might have seen me at different times in different forms, but I am eternally the same Soul.

Because I am the Mother of Jesus Christ, and because we are all one in Christ, I am your Mother, too. I am much more than a historical figure who lived in a particular country at a particular time. I am a figurehead of Woman, of Motherhood, of Nurturing.

But I am not a goddess and I do not wish to be seen as a goddess, nor thought of that way. I am not about primitive energy. I am about refined, disciplined energy. I am an evolved teacher, a mediatrix of great responsibility. And I am – like you – a perfect Child of God. Also, I am – like you – perfectly loving. Like the Christ, and like you, I am Love. I am part of the God-energy, as are you.

Because you and I are both Children of God, each of us has a responsibility to each other. Each of us is called to be a nurturer of our brothers and sisters. Each of us in time is called to be a teacher. We are all going back to the Father together. So it is our joint mission to share Love and Light with each of our brothers. We will all be deprived of the ultimate Joy of Heaven until each last Soul has chosen the Light. That is why I am here to help hasten this process.

Thus, it is questionable why you would lock up some of your brothers and sisters in jail, indefinitely, without being merciful and loving to them. You will have to eventually become their brother, sister, and teacher in the long run. So why delay this process? Do your best to encourage their spiritual growth when they are in prison. It is often an ideal time for them to make Soul progress while they are confined. At such time they are not as distracted by the world. And oftentimes their hearts have become very repentant, sorrowful and compassionate. Share my book with them if their hearts are open.

The message my Son came down to share 2,000 years ago was simple and clear: *Love one another as your Father has loved you.* We are all One. Each Soul is part of a beautiful Whole. And, together, we are the catalysts who will bring this to fruition.

MOTHER OF GRACE

I am honored by all the titles you, my Children, have given me over the centuries. Mary was my name. Virgin referred to me in my human life as a more temporal term. Blessed is an endearing word of honor that I thank you for applying to me. Blessed Virgin Mary. But that is an inappropriate, old title for me. It is the old way that many people saw me for centuries. You may still use that name and see me with a halo and down-turned eyes. That is how many artists depicted me. It was as if my major mission was to be holy. But that is such a limited view of me.

I need to be seen in a new way in this new era. I am not a person of down-turned eyes, waiting to be praised for my holiness. I am a woman who would rather look directly into your eyes – with Love.

So I would like you to think of me as MARY, MOTHER OF GRACE. That title comes the closest to embodying who and what I am. Mothering, Nurturing and Loving are my mission. And Grace is what I bring as part of my Light. So, Mary, Mother of Grace, or Our Mother of Grace, is a title that I truly love. It means so much to me in terms of how I can relate to each of you — and to your Children — in this life. It is how I want you to think of me. And I am here to share with you how your life can become a beautiful, simple miracle.

BEING FRIENDS

You ask how you can be close to me and be my friend. You can read this book. You can think about it. You can talk about it. You can talk about me. You can treat me as a loving friend. You can pray intimately with me whenever you want. You can appreciate my quiet presence with you. That is how we can build our friendship.

Best of all, you can show Love to all the Children of God. That means everyone! You can demonstrate Love in your life. You can play. You can laugh. You can be happy. All those things honor me.

Remember that I am not a medieval or an ancient Virgin Mother. I am as alive today as you are. I live in the moment, just as I encourage you to live in the moment. That is the only place you will find life. You will never find the real me in the past, for I no longer dwell there. My true energies are always with you in the Present Moment.

THE NEW MILLENNIUM

For you, it probably seems like much time has elapsed since my lifetime on earth with Jesus. Let me assure you that, on the plane where I am, 2,000 years is not such a long time. And I have been busy with many nurturing responsibilities.

But a new era is upon us, and this new millennium that is opening up before us is going to be a great time, symbolically. It will be a time for Love and for outreach. I am just beginning to come into my more serious responsibilities on your planet.

In the new millennium, especially as we get into its spirit after the first ten to twenty years, you will see a great change coming over the earth. As your Spiritual Mother, my energies will grow stronger and begin to be noticed more and more. Both men and women will experience the gentler, loving energies of their nature. There will be great Peace; Love will prevail over the earth. I am here to start directing that flow of energy. Those Souls who are of a more warring or violent nature will find it uncomfortable to live out their darkness surrounded by people of Light. They will choose to leave our loving earth and to return only when they are ready to learn to Love.

We will be moving into a time of Light – greater than the golden age of Greece or the age of cathedral building, or the Renaissance. It will be a time of great beauty and strength and Love. Churches will flourish. Art, Music, Dance and the Language Arts will flourish. Most of the ugliness and strife that reared its mean energy in the 1900s – world wars, violence, crime, separation – will diminish and eventually dissolve to a mere shadow of what they were.

In the new millennium your police will be helping to build better communities rather than having to focus on crime. Your health workers will be focusing on achieving higher levels of health, rather than coping with illness and disease.

This third millennium will be a millennium of Light. My Son, Jesus Christ, is most grateful for this. You will see more and more of us as time progresses and as the Light grows. We are here to spread Love and to lead as Lightbearers. The timing simply had to be right for all of this to occur.

I know that many of you are discouraged because of the violence you see around you. Let me remind you again that what you focus on becomes your reality. If you look for violence, you will see violence. And if you look for Love, you will see Love. These are decisions of the heart, and you are barely aware of the great power you have in you to create – to create a world of Love, rather than fear.

Your responsibility, as we move into this new era, will be to create a loving atmosphere where my Son's teachings will flourish. His Truths will not pass away. They are coming to pass in all their beauty and grandeur.

What you call the New Testament is now about to be lived. The dragons of greed, war and lust are growing old and tired. Your responsibility is to turn your attention away from whatever still exists of the era of fear. Do not give it attention. Do not focus on it and it will dissolve into nothingness. Ignore television programs and films that focus on the ugly and dark side of people. Do not fight them. Choose instead to focus on beauty and strength.

Nurture your Children to be interested in Beauty and Truth. The Children now being born have great leadership abilities and are here to help us move into the Light Millennium. Help them to keep their innocence. Discipline the extent of television and electronic illusions they are exposed to. Try to keep them in our real world of Love instead of in an artificial, illusory world.

Television is creating an emptiness, a passivity, a loneliness in the Souls of many of my Children across the world. Television is but an illusion of a life experience. While it has the advantage of sharing knowledge and laughter, it is not a substitute for human interaction. I feel sadness in my heart about this. Television is the great separator and illusion-maker of your era. It can also eat up much of your time. It can become an excuse for life, and so I ask you to limit its use in your lives. Get out – shake hands – smile – hug one another! Live life to its fullest. Do not be afraid to open up your hearts to one another. Drop the fears that keep you separated. In this you will be opening yourself to a fuller life, a real life. And you will feel the joy.

Most of all, you will begin to dissolve the depression that is so pervasive in today's world. To live only in a world of illusion is a very depressing way to spend a lifetime. Go to your churches, your associations, places where you can contribute with your brothers and sisters to make a difference in this world.

Part Two

Living A Life Of Love

A LIFE OF LOVE IS A LIFE OF EXPERIENCE. IT IS A LIFE OF MAKING THE right choices. It is a life of choosing Love, choosing happiness. So many people think that the important thing is to be right. It is not. The important thing is to be happy! Being right and being happy are often diametrically opposed. Being happy means being flexible, not rigid.

Being "right" all the time is tiring, serious, and a thankless thought process. As I mentioned before, we got into the earth predicament originally by taking ourselves too seriously. I would like my Children to stop trying to be "right" about everything. There is too much seriousness on your planet.

To be "right" is often to be righteous. This is not the way to happiness. Nor is it the way to live a life of Love. Try to evaluate your old decision to be right. The important thing is this: *Are all your decisions made with Love?*

Those of my Children who play the "serious" game are often doing it because of fear. Fear stems from that idea of punishment. If the earth is a place where God's Children came to hide from Him (and there is a certain Truth to this), there is a great fear of punishment still alive in the world. But this is not where the evolution of your life should be going. Being "right" and "serious" is where we were in the past. Today's lesson is not about covering yourself by being right about everything.

Try to reevaluate this old decision to be right. No one cares – least of all God or Jesus or myself – whether you are "right" or not. Is there Love in your heart? I would like to see you give yourselves and each other the gift of happiness. This requires a disciplined, new way of thinking.

A life of Love and happiness is a life of wonderment and gratitude for all the incredible opportunities that surround you. In each day there are an infinite number of opportunities for giving, for outreach. This is the point of life.

Yet what do so many people do? They build walls of separation so they will not have to give. They are afraid of giving because they are afraid of exposing themselves, because they are afraid of rejection, because they invent reasons why they are in danger. Perhaps they funnel themselves into a little world and adopt a little routine. They interact with a little circle of people. Perhaps they take on a little sickness and nurture it into a major illness. In their leisure time they eat, sleep, watch TV, and stay locked up. But is this life?

As your Mother, I must ask all of you to open yourselves to the new experiences of life. If life does not readily present these experiences for you – create them for yourselves!

LIVE A LIFE OF OUTREACH

You have a precious opportunity, being here on earth. Open your doors. Go out. Meet people. Go to your churches. Have fellowship. Look other people in the eye. Laugh. Cry. Smile. Wake up. Have feelings. Have new experiences. I urge you to come alive for your own sake. Too many of my Children are wasting their precious lives in a dim, gray state.

In addition to happiness, another important ingredient to a life of Love is Joy, Joy of living, Joy of Loving. This is what was so great about my Son, Jesus. He had this tremendous Joy. People followed Him around because of His Joy. They didn't know what it was. But it was a passion for living, for being with others, for giving, for extension. Joy comes from gratitude. Joy comes from thankfulness for who you are. Joy comes from knowing who your Heavenly Father is, who your Brother is (my Son), and who your family is (everyone!).

When you live a life of Love you will live in Joy. You will live in the Present Moment. You will have dropped the past. You will not be worried about the future. You will realize that the only moment you truly have is this Present Moment. And in it, you will rejoice! You will be able to celebrate life.

THE WORLD OF TODAY: ABUNDANCE & STARVATION

Today's world is a very trying, unnerving experience for many people. Many Souls take today's world very seriously, and to those Souls the world can be a very insane place – because it is based on fear. People are afraid for their safety, afraid of their health, afraid they won't have enough...It is an insane way to see the world, and it is not based on Love.

The world is such a strange environment. Never has there been more material abundance...Such silliness in food, cars, clothes and toys for both children and adults! There is great excess in your world.

And still there are so many hungry children and financially hurting adults living in debt. I am saddened by the limitation and monetary tightness in which so many of you find yourselves. Many of you do not see the inequities. We need compassion for the underdog. There are always opportunities for the strong to help the weak.

There is no lack in the world. There is more food produced than could ever be used. But it is not spread around and shared. Politics and greed keep food from the mouths of hungry Children of God. It is a travesty that ANY Child should go hungry in such an abundant world. So much is produced, but much of it never reaches the hands of my little and big Children. Many still go to bed hungry in this modern age and that is a travesty. This is because of the insanity of the world and its selfish values. My Children should first concern themselves that everyone is fed and cared for. That is supportive of the human dignity that each Soul deserves.

You live in a world where there is everything, and yet there is nothing. Do not live in the illusions of your world. Return to the values of Love and the Heart. Return to your churches. Return to your families. Return to your friends. Heal the separation, and you can create your own Heaven on earth. This is the only way back to your Father: decisions of the Heart, decisions of Love, decisions of Union and Oneness. With decisions of Love, prejudice will dissolve, and the Holy Spirit will quietly, surely, help bring you to the forgiveness in your heart that makes us one family again. And so will I.

Never forget that the Holy Spirit is working in each of you, every moment, to give you the next lesson, the next chance to decide for Love. He is the Answer that the Father has sent to heal your brokenness. Feel His Presence in your Soul. It is closer than your breathing.

I, too, will help you. I will show you how to do this, how to move gradually from separation to Joy, in the next few years. Stay with me and I will help light your path for you.

You are so blessed. You are so loved. It is not your destiny to suffer. The Holy Spirit is with you to bring you to a place of Comfort, Joy and Peace. He will bring you there through Love. He is so gentle, so very patient. I am here to help Him accomplish this mission of Love.

THE EVOLUTION OF YOUR LIFE

As I mentioned earlier, I am here to help you open your heart.

I also said that I was here to help you with the evolution of your life. By this I mean an opening of the Soul to its own authenticity.

Here are some important concepts that I want you to be aware of as you move through your life:

First, Our Heavenly Father made each Soul in His likeness, but each of you reflects a different part of Him, an individual perfect part of God, so each of you is *special*. I am not referring to *certain people as special,* but to *everyone as special*. This is an important concept for you to grasp, because it will help reduce prejudice and judgment.

Much of the fluff of the world is about being special – homes, cars, clothes, money. Even sickness is often about being special. Specialness is a trap. It is based on the belief that some people are better than others. People affix value to being more special than others. But this is false specialness.

Authentic specialness is seeing yourself as the perfect, integrated Being that you are, just the way that God made you. Authentic specialness means that you can see God in everyone at any time. This is also known as seeing the Christ in others.

Getting to see yourself as authentically special means that you value yourself for the right reasons, and this gives you integrity. You feel good about yourself for the right reasons, and time cannot take your integrity away from you.

Second, I want to help you see that whatever happens in your life has usually been the perfect occurrence, the perfect lesson, for that point in time. Regardless of what occurred in your life, it was always the perfect vehicle to get you to your next level of experience. These happenings are arranged by you and your Inner Teacher, the Holy Spirit. You are never forced to choose a lesson that is against your will. You are never forced to choose a lesson you do not want. Anything that happens to you is subconsciously agreed upon, even if it seems inconvenient, inopportune or painful.

As you begin to get used to this perception, then as you look at yourself, your loved ones or other people, you will begin to be able to see how things that happened in life were often the perfect experience for you to evolve.

Most importantly, you will see yourself and others as perfect, just the way you are. Even with all your little or big human imperfections, underneath you are always a perfect Child of God. You never lose your innocence. You may think you have. But, because you are created by God in his image, you can never be less than perfect. Ugliness or failure or loss is just a surface illusion.

Third, the old idea of suffering as a way of evolvement is not enlightened thinking. It is time to let go of the idea that suffering or martyrdom is noble. It is nothing more than suffering or martyrdom. And, at that, it is not a very good choice. Learning through pain and suffering is an old, tired way of learning your life lessons. Some people cannot learn by any other method because they choose to learn through suffering. But this is not being loving to yourself.

Start to learn by Love, not through pain. You do have the choice.

Fourth, you are not a victim. God is not playing you like a puppet. You are creating your own life. And you are responsible for creating your own life. This may be hard for you to grasp because it involves being responsible for everything you do. Not everyone likes that much responsibility, but it is the Truth. And in your evolvement, you will eventually have to face it. The sooner you face it, the more powerful you will become.

Fifth, when you grasp the fact that you have Free Will, that you are Love, that no one is holding you back, everything becomes possible. Then, life is just a matter of deciding what you want to accomplish. At this point, the boxes of your thinking begin to dissolve. You begin to see that all is Love. That God is about expansiveness, and so are you. And that there is nothing to be afraid of. That is a big step.

At this point, you achieve Heaven on earth! And I am here to show you how each of you can live a life of Heaven, right here on earth.

When you become inspired to see your own perfection, your own value, you begin to see your own possibilities for greatness. You were not created by God to live a small or meaningless life. You were each meant to be expansive and happy. Each of you has a meaningful and happy destiny.

DECISIONS BASED ON FEAR

Wherever you are on earth is a choosing ground. You are on earth to make an important choice many times each day — Love or fear.

You have Free Will, so you may make whatever decision you choose. But if you choose fear, the same lesson will keep repeating until you get the answer right. It is very boring to be stuck in life with the same problems repeating again and again. When you are tired of the repetition, remember: The answer is always Love. And apparently you have not made the right decision for Love, and so the problem keeps repeating.

When you choose fear, you choose limitation; you choose separation. You choose sickness and suffering. And ultimately you choose death. The world is very complex and structured around fear, so it takes considerable courage and discipline to rise above fear. This is a disciplined process and I am here to help you rise above the old, fearful ways of thinking.

The world teaches the fear system of thought. Fear can be a great motivator. But it is in opposition to your Father – who is Love.

You are here on earth to learn to join with your Father. Since you left Him, paradoxically speaking, in the Garden, you have had a long path. And many of your decisions since that time were based on fear – fear of having done the wrong thing, fear that you offended your Father, fear of scarcity, fear of sickness, and fear of death.

As you have evolved from primitive to civilized Souls, more and more of your decisions have been based on Love. Slowly, systematically, you have begun to choose Love, to teach Love, for Love is what you are.

When I talk about Love, I am talking about the "outward stroke." Let us call it the outward stroke because it means reaching out, joining. It is the creative stroke – helping, serving, joining with God.

The inward stroke is just the opposite. Let us think of it as the selfish stroke – inward, for self alone, scarcity, protection, walling off. This was the stroke of primitive man, of isolationism, of war, of everything that has plagued man since the figurative separation in the Garden of Eden.

Of course, man never really separated from God. He cannot because God is all Love and total joining. But man chose fear and created a separating dream. And that separating dream is what earth is all about.

My purpose in this communication as your caring, nurturing Mother of Grace is to let you know that the outward stroke includes me. When you make a decision based on Love, you are joining with me and with your Father and my Son. In addition, the Holy Spirit is always with you (whether you are aware of it or not). And so are all the angels and Souls of the firmament.

And when you choose the outward stroke there is an added benefit. You choose Grace, and Grace is a superb gift. Grace is like a mantle of ease that surrounds you. It is a total gift that keeps you safe, that keeps you free, yet protected. Too few of my Children are aware of the presence of Grace in their lives and how it helps them. I am here to point out the difference between Grace and suffering.

It bears repeating: *You may choose to learn in either of two ways*:

1. *Through suffering*
2. *Through Grace*

Suffering is totally unnecessary. You may not have known it, but as your Spiritual Mother, I am telling you that now. You may forget suffering. You may forget pain. You may choose to learn your life lessons through Grace. Your life will be vastly simpler, more beautiful, and more filled with Love; this is as it should be. When you live by Grace it nurtures a part of you called Innocence. This is part of your true heritage.

When you pass away, it is not necessary to die from an illness or an accident. You can gracefully die in your bed, or in a chair, quietly and peacefully. That is a more graceful choice.

DECISIONS BASED ON LOVE

You live in a world often dominated by a kind of "mass hypnosis." There is a "right" way of seeing things and a "wrong" way. The "right" way is the way that most people have been conditioned to think. As an example, there may be a flu virus in your area. Many people may fear the virus. They may believe that if someone with the virus sneezes on them they will have a very strong chance of catching it. They do not want the virus, but if they keep thinking about it, fearing it, they, of course, will probably attract the virus and get the very thing they least wanted. How did this happen? The Law of Attraction says: *Whatever you focus on expands.* This is a creative act. When you think about viruses, you attract more viruses. When you think about fear, you attract more fear. This is part of the hypnosis under which you live.

How could you approach this differently? When you hear there is a virus "going around," you may decide that you do not want it. You decide that you see no value in the process of getting sick. You decide that is not where you are – it is not the lesson you want.

Instead, you become clear that you love yourself and, therefore, you decide not to become sick. And, thus, you do not attract sickness. Fear never enters your heart. You do not see yourself as the victim of a germ or a sneeze or tiredness or anything weak. This gives you an entirely new strata of decisions on which to base your life. It will give you freedom from mass hypnosis. It feels good to be free. Enjoy the freedom this will bring. But as I told you, this takes a new, disciplined way of thinking. It means changing your mind about the way you see things. You could call it "The Mary Way."

This is what I mean by a decision based on Love. You Love and respect yourself, so why would you inflict sickness on yourself? You begin to choose ways to be nice to yourself, ways to make yourself happy. This is not selfish. It is honest. When you do this with Love, it brings you more and more happiness. And, once you love yourself, you are more capable of loving others.

To free yourself, you need to go through a process of Undoing with the Holy Spirit. He will help you, as will I. We will help you achieve a basic simplicity in your heart, a place where a simple prayer has great meaning for you – a simple meal with a friend, a simple walk. Simple things can be a great Joy. When there is gratefulness in your heart, you can look out the window at the start of a new day and feel great Joy, realizing, "This is a day that was made for Love!" You can decide to make all decisions with Love in your heart.

And that, my beautiful Children, is what you need to get back to. Many of you are off-center now. You feel lost. Life may have no real "point." You may feel less and less satisfaction. You may ask of life – Is this all there is?

No, it is not all there is. That is a "jaded" way of seeing life – when life, as you know it, ceases to have deep, heartfelt meaning.

I am writing this book to my Children, for while many of you have the idea already, many others do not. To those of you who do, I want you to keep teaching others what you already know in your heart. Many of you have that centeredness, that simplicity, that innocence of heart that others are yearning for.

You can teach other people how to get there. That is your calling, your talent in life. Help to show others the shift necessary to live with joy and happiness. Many people want to learn this. Share it.

You can share through my books, my Mary Evenings, my Mary Gardens. There will be many ways. I will share more about this with you later in this book. You are an important part of this vision, this celestial speedup that my Son Jesus refers to -- in order to wake people up from their current "sleep."

There are several aspects to our initial work together, my Children. The first is this book and my continuing message to you. I am not going to speak to you once on these topics and then disappear from earth for another fifty years. I am going to be a continuing leader of this project and I will not fade from sight. You can depend on my presence and focus. I will also depend on yours.

I am here to help clear a pathway for all my Children, and to help them achieve purity of heart. My way will be clear and simple, and it will help you to be able to live life based on decisions made through Love, rather than fear.

While my continuity may have originally come from the Catholic Church, remember that I am a Spiritual Mother to the world. I am here for each of you, regardless of your religion. You now live in an ecumenical age where the brotherhood of man is accepted. Separation is dissolving. This is a step closer to heaven. This spiritual pathway from your Mother of Grace should be shared with Protestants, Catholics, Jews, Mormons, Buddhists, Hindus, Bahais, Moslems – every one of my Children regardless of denomination.

My new role is not about the time-honored concept of "religion." I am here for the sake of your spirituality. You will see as I communicate with you that my message is not a dictation on what to "believe." It is neither historical nor political. It is a way to SEE life. It is about living from the heart, living with LOVE.

Envision me as your Spiritual Mother, because my mother energy and nurturing is much needed in this world to achieve what my Son, Jesus Christ, has laid out for us.

THE GIFT OF INNOCENCE

Whatever you think you might have done in the Garden of Eden does not change the fact that each of you is a perfect Child of God. God did not create your Soul in error. He created you as a perfect Child of God. That means that perfect innocence is second nature to you. You may not change what God created. Never think of yourself as second class, or as tainted. As a Child of God you are first class. Innocence is the state in which God created you. And innocence is what you still are.

You are a perfect Child of God learning the perfect lessons for your development. However much you might hate the idea of being perfect – and of learning the perfect lesson – this is Truth. This is how your Heavenly Father sees you. You are basically perfect and there is absolutely nothing you can do about it!

The idea of original sin was simple. The sin was not choosing Love. The sin was departing from your Father with fear. The sin was hiding. But you did not hurt your Father through this dream. He is perfect Love. Your Father is Love itself, and to Him no sin is unforgivable.

Please begin to let go of any ideas about your taintedness. God made you innocent and pure. No matter how old you grow, no matter how many sicknesses and injuries may have tired you out, in your Soul you are innocent and pure and free. You are now, and will always be, a perfect Child of God.

Knowing that you are innocent at your very core means that you can now begin to work through the layers of guilt that undoubtedly keep you down. It means that you can live without the fear of sickness and death. If you are innocent, what is there to fear? When you come to the point where you realize your innocence, you can begin to see and accept the Grace that surrounds you.

What I am telling you may seem simplistic, but it is a wonderful message. It is a message of Hope and Love. I want you to be able to reach the point of innocence where you can get silly, happy, funny, joyous and playful. There is real health there and that is how I want you and all my Children to be. I know you are capable of choosing seriousness – but can you choose silliness and rejoice in it? My message to you is simple: *lighten up*, have fun in life. You can still do this while being responsible. But remember to laugh, and remember how to play.

DEPRESSION

Depression is a sickness of the heart. It comes from guilt, from sadness, from emptiness. Sometimes it comes from doing all the right things for the wrong reasons.

Depression also comes from limited hope. It comes from not seeing yourself as the perfect Child of God that you are. It also comes from a sense of separation... from feeling trapped. It comes from a feeling of "What's the use?" It can come from not having a point to your life. It can come from being too much of an adult and not enough of a Child.

Depression is rampant in your society today. And no one need feel ashamed of having the problem. It is easier to admit it and to seek a solution than to be stuck in denial and afraid to admit your feelings of depression. This subject is too important to be taken casually. It needs focused attention. I will be there to help you through this. In the near future I will provide a guided audiotape that you can work on to overcome this limitation. You can use new systems such as bioresonance to help dissolve these old thought processes. But try not to use drugs as an answer. Ask me for my Grace in helping you to cope with depression. I am always here for you.

EVERYDAY MIRACLES

My Children, miracles are part of the very fabric of your life. Miracles are a new way of seeing things. Miracles are a way of seeing life through the eyes of the Holy Spirit and through the eyes of Christ.

The usual meaning of the word "miracle" is more like a miraculous healing, as Jesus Christ did so many times during his life on earth. Those miracles involved phenomena that changed some physical aspect of the universe. That was the old-fashioned way of seeing miracles.

The new way of seeing miracles is much subtler. You can see miracles around you all the time – if you are observant.

The higher your spiritual discipline, the closer you are to the Light…the easier it is to see miracles all around you.

Miracles are a new way of seeing – seeing through the eyes of the Holy Spirit or the eyes of Christ. You see the same old things you have always seen – friends, relatives, work, life, yourself – in an entirely new dimension. It is like an enormous AHA! But it often happens a step at a time.

Someone who works consistently to be on a higher spiritual plane will see life in an entirely new light. A life that otherwise seemed drab, boring, unpromising – seen through the eyes of the miracle – breathes an entirely new life!

There are many aspects to miracles. They are everyone's right. Everyone is special. Everyone is a Child of God. Miracles are for ALL God's Children with no exceptions. Miracles are natural. NOT to see them is unnatural. It is important to know that miracles are everyone's right, but you have to go through a period of purification to regularly see and live them.

By purification I mean forgiveness of others and self. Letting go of judgment. Undoing the old ways of seeing life – especially the small, limited ways of seeing life and yourself. This is a process taught by *A Course in Miracles* that my Son, Jesus Christ, gave to the world over twenty-five years ago. It is not a magic path, but it is a very enlightened path. I am sharing some of His same principles put in a much simpler way. This is what He asked me to do for you.

A Course in Miracles is very much a spiritual discipline. It is a new way of spiritual thinking. It brings you to a state of spiritual discipline where you become honest with yourself. You have to "call yourself" when you see yourself gravitating back to your old habits of thinking. With it, you begin to see the world through a new set of eyes – the eyes of Christ.

A small contingent of Souls has studied *A Course in Miracles*. The book is in most bookstores. It is translated into many languages. It is a very thorough course which facilitates the "Undoing" process. I will try to share with you a few more of its principles in this book.

Most Souls don't begin to SEE the world through the eyes of miracles all at once. It is a re-education of all your values. For instance, whenever you are sick, you seldom become healed until you decide deep down within yourself that you are sick and tired of being sick. And so you make a decision for wellness. The decision is made with the Holy Spirit. At that moment, the miracle has occurred. The body might not catch up to the "wellness" for a short period of time, until the cells adjust. But the actual miracle takes place at the time you decided with your Holy Spirit, or Higher Self, to be well – to join with all Spirit.

Here is another example of a miracle: You have some people in your life who truly bother you – very deeply. When you are in their presence you are fearful and emotional. There might be a deep hurt. When you begin to see those people through the eyes of Love you might see them as a catalyst to your own healing because they bring up something in you that needs healing. You might begin to see them through the eyes of Love, realizing that the Holy Spirit lives in them, too, and that they, too, are Children of God. You might see the Christ in them. You might begin to see them as a sister or brother. You might begin to feel at peace in their presence. This is a miracle in process. Even people who have pushed your emotional "hot buttons" for years – when seen through the eyes of the miracle – can be unthreatening to you. This is because you have healed within and you now attract like energies from without. And so you are free, and happier for it.

In each of these instances, the miracle is happening – not within the world – but within yourself. As you begin to see life differently, so will others see you differently and react to you in an entirely new way. Life is about making miracles.

Each day is made for miracles. Miracles are part of the very fabric of life. It is your decision about choosing to see life in a new way that brings the miracle to you. It will bring you happiness and lightness of heart. You will feel joyous and very lucky.

I would like to offer you the benefit and Grace of seeing me as your helper in this process of learning to live life in miracles. You may call on me, or pray to me – even call me your Mother of Miracles. I will always be there for you. At any moment of the night or day.

Part Three

Taking The Time To Pray

MY CHILDREN, NEVER BELIEVE FOR A MOMENT THAT THERE IS NO value in prayer. Prayer is a statement. Prayer enriches. Prayer strengthens. Prayer says that you believe in something bigger than yourself. It says that you believe in the inter-connectedness of God and the Sonship.

Prayer is about your intent. And it can have great power. Weak prayer may produce weak results. But strong prayers produce strong results. Miracles play an important part in how you LOOK for answers to your prayers. Blessed are those who believe before they see. There is a saying, "You'll see it when you believe it." There is much Truth in that statement.

The power and strength of prayer is created by you. The moment you pray and SEE IT SO, it is. It may take some time for the physical manifestation to emerge, but it already IS on the creative, or God level.

What you cannot see when you pray is the vast interconnectedness of the

Sonship working at infinite levels.

There is no prayer that goes unanswered if you pray with deep sincerity and honesty of heart. Be steadfast in your prayers. And realize that the prayer itself is an important part of the gift.

Even though your prayers have been answered, there will often be answers that may go unrecognized. You may not recognize the unusualness of the answer that may be right before your very eyes. You may not be ready for the miracle-solution that is staring you in the face.

THE ROSARY

I still have a very strong tie with Souls through the Rosary. No, there are not as many people praying it today as in times past. People who pray the Rosary often have very humble, open hearts – hearts like Children. The repetitive prayers of the Rosary make it like a meditative prayer – which can be very relaxing. It takes time to say the Rosary.

There are so many people with deep, abiding Love who pray the Rosary all the time. It takes a disciplined mind to do the Rosary well. But it is a lovely and very beautiful prayer. Remember: the prayer is not so much for God, or for me, as it is for the person DOING the praying.

The Rosary is simple. It is comforting. It affirms some of the greatest Truths of your spiritual existence here on earth. Say it very slowly. Let the meaning sink in.

I encourage you to live the Rosary and say it often. It has deep meaning for all of us as a family united in the Father and in Christ, my Son. I pray that you will use it – often.

With regard to Rosaries, I would prefer that they no longer be made with the symbol of the dying Jesus Christ on the cross at the apex. I would much prefer to see a symbol of the resurrected Jesus Christ, the Prince of Peace. That is who he really is, the Prince of Peace. The dying Christ on the cross is not a good symbol for life or Love. It dwells on the wrong part of my Son's life. Try to picture Jesus Christ as a man of strength, clarity, conviction – a great teacher – and a truly Noble Son of God. That was My Son, Jesus Christ. That is how He should be remembered.

MY CATHOLIC CHURCH

Has there been any other church where I have been more closely embraced and honored over the centuries than the Catholic Church? I think not. The Catholic Church has kept the memory of me alive in the hearts of the people over the centuries through the devotions, the Rosary, the cathedrals built in my honor, the universities and schools named after me. Catholics have kept me alive in the world and in their hearts and I am honored. Would not any mother be honored by the loyalty and Love these Children have shown me? I am. While I am not "owned" by the Catholic Church, I am grateful for its support and I surround the entity of the Catholic Church with Love and Light as I have for centuries and millenniums – since its inception. But I am a Mother to all of mankind. I am a Universal Mother. And so I have no single church to which I belong. I am beyond churches. I embrace all churches that operate with Love as their foundation.

INSPIRED WRITINGS

The Bible is a miraculous resource; be grateful to have it intact after all these centuries. But it is important to realize that the Bible was written almost 2,000 years ago. The Old and New Testaments were written, not by God, but by men. They are inspired writings. But they are old inspired writings.

The sad thing about sacred scripture is that the Fathers of the Church did not continue to add to those inspired writings. They froze those writings in time. Let me assure you that man and his Soul is not frozen in time. Let me also assure you that there is a great difference in the civilization that lived 2,000 years ago and the civilization that lives today. Souls have evolved. Consciousness has evolved. The learning orientation is different. My Children need new material for the age in which they live.

Of course, it was a "safe" decision to cap off inspired writings many centuries ago. It was a way of safeguarding the Bible as a repository of Truth. But this decision was made long ago. Today we live in an era of information and publishing. Consider that churches could be assembling a new body of inspired writings – of today. Unfortunately there are not writings by Jesus Christ in the Bible, except for a few phrases attributed to Him. It is time that His new writings be assembled and honored. This would give my Children another new area of Truth from which to learn.

Jesus Christ is resurrected and He is still very much alive and with us. That is the whole point of the Resurrection. Jesus Christ is still alive and communicating today. But, except for a few enlightened people, few are listening to what He has to say today. What He is saying today is more relevant to today's world than some of His gospels of the past. His recent book, *Dialogue on Awakening* (by Tom Carpenter) should be discovered and enjoyed by many more people, if they truly love and honor Jesus Christ. Be open to the current words of Jesus Christ on a continuing basis if you believe in the Living Christ. Another of Jesus' recent communications is *Reflections of the Christ Mind* (by Paul Ferrini). These are gifts He gave you for your current age.

That is why I am here, communicating to you through this book – to remind you that we are very much alive in consciousness, and we are still bringing you words of Love and inspiration. It will be our role to do this throughout eternity. It will be your role to be open to and accepting of our word.

WOMEN AS PRIESTS IN THE CATHOLIC CHURCH

We have just finished a millennium that has been very male-dominated. The masculine energy took control for a long time. In this period there has been much achievement. There have also been many wars. There has been much suffering. There has been much abuse of children and of women, as well as men. We have now ended that millennium. This new millennium in which we are now living will be much different. It will be a millennium of female energy, of learning through Love, of nurturing, of Forgiveness, of coming into our Whole Integrated Selves.

There will come a time – not too far into the new millennium, perhaps another generation or two – when women will be invited to be priests in the Catholic Church. This will be presented to them as an honor and they will accept it with dignity, and be superb at it. It is all a matter of time. It is an evolvement.

The clergy that have held the line against this up until now have been acting from their own sense of Truth, their own tradition. They did right in their own eyes. The new clergy coming in the next 25, 50, 100 years will be grounded in a new Truth, a new tradition. The Catholic Church will follow suit, as have other churches, and will open up to the Truth that all sexes are equal in the eyes of God. They will understand that God does not have a gender; that God is not a man, and has no prejudice or preference toward gender, be they men or women.

It is important to remember that each human Soul has both male and female energy centers within. That is why I mentioned that you are each complete within yourself. Males have a soft side and a hard side. Females have a soft side and a hard side. In the new millennium there will be more respect for the softer, yin energy that is more open, more understanding, more accepting.

When I say that this will be a millennium of female energy, of learning through Love...I am refering to the female energy of both men and women...their soft side, their loving, nurturing side.

This will engender an era of acceptance, an era of gentleness. Both men and women will build relationships easily. Many of the old separations and games and contentions will dissolve. Forgiveness will bring about a new era of friendship, of exchange, of a beautiful Oneness among all my Children all over the globe. It is already happening. More and more of the world's old fears will dissolve. Women will have much to do with this new spirituality.

Also, men will not be so threatened by women. Men living in the field of Love will accept the natural abilities of each Soul and not judge capabilities based on gender. That is why women will become priests in most of the major churches of the world by the end of this century.

Men will be able to share church responsibilities without fear. The idea of sacred orders for men only will slowly dissolve, and upcoming generations of Children will never know the old prejudices of the past.

The New World of the millennium will be a New World based on Love. I will help lead you there. I will help you grow into this.

LEARNING TO LIVE LOVE

Earth is not the be-all and end-all of your existence. It is an important part of your process of re-enlightenment. You are here on earth for a very important reason. It comes down to something rather simple. I am going to tell it to you once and I want this to stand out.

**The purpose of life is for you to learn
to make decisions based on Love rather than fear.**

The world is full of Souls who still do the right things for the wrong reasons. They often perform loving acts out of fear of what might happen if they did not. When you learn to make true decisions out of Love, you will have accomplished the point of life.

Love is what you are.

This is being true to Self. You were created by God as a veritable spark of the Divine. You all have a noble and a Divine heritage. As God's Children, you were created of the same substance of God Himself – and that is Love. When your spiritual path takes you to the point where you work through all the layers of fear down to the essence of your heart and Soul...what you will find there is Love.

Love is what you are. So choose to think Love. Act Love. Decide Love. Be Love. And your life will change. You will Love totally in Grace. Your life will be dramatically different and you will experience great peace in your heart. It will be like Heaven on earth. And you will know not only happiness, but Joy itself, which is close to the emotion you experience when you are in the presence of and close to God.

My Son, Jesus Christ, sent me on a mission to you. In spite of all the advances there have been on earth – people helping people – higher standards of living, improved communications – He is asking again for a celestial speedup.

By this He means that Souls in the world are not making enough progress. The ego is usually going nowhere, fast. For all of the superfluous activity of life (and you human beings are a busy group!) you are not always getting closer to completion. At your current rate of advance you and your children may be repeating remedial experiences here on earth for a long, long time.

I would like my Children to focus more consistently on why they are here...*on what their lessons are in life.*

You have a lifetime here on earth. It is a very, very precious commodity. There are untold numbers of Souls who would like to occupy your place on earth because you can make great progress on the earth plane. Your life here is a chance to live Love. To make decisions based on Love – that is the whole point of existence. Once you begin to focus on the heart of the matter you can make great progress.

WORKING WITH THE EGO

One of the deterrents to your progress here on earth is a little aspect we refer to as the "ego." The ego is an old part of your nature, the old part of you that is built on fear. The ego seems very prudent, because it is always fussing, posturing, and worrying. The ego is the fearful side of you. Everyone on earth has an ego. How you decide to handle your ego is everything.

The ego always wants to keep you in limitation, in bondage. It wants to be in control. But you must not give it control. And you must not buy into its fear. As your Mother-nurturer I remind you that it is very important to have an awareness of your ego. Without that awareness, you can stay stuck in life for very long periods. Yet, when you have an awareness of how your ego is victimizing you, you are then free to make changes.

It might be helpful for you to think of your ego as a little, unruly child. Your ego can be very conniving; it can also be sneaky. At times it can pretend to be very good. This can sometimes be very hard to discern.

As you grow in wisdom and Grace, you will understand that the ego needs to be disciplined and held in control, much as you have to rein in and control an undisciplined child. This is a side of your nature that keeps you from perfect Love and perfect Peace.

Therefore, if you are to make progress here on earth, you need to have a way of handling your ego. Recognize its voice as the first to speak inside you, the first to have an opinion, the first to fear. The ego cares desperately about being "right." It is the cowardly side of you that is more interested in protecting itself, its own interests and its own agenda.

Do not give your power to your ego. Maintain control at all times. You might listen to the ego's point of view, then say to yourself, "Thank you for sharing." In other words, you rein it in. And you continue with your loving Higher Self in control.

The difference here is that the ego will always want to run the show in your life. It is your selfish side. It will act out of fear. It is the part of you that wants to be special all the time. But it is not the real You. The real You is loving, noble, generous, happy, and fearless. That is the part of you that you want to see more and more of.

HOW TO WORK WITH THE HOLY SPIRIT

There is a part of you, your true self, your Higher Self, that has an Inner Teacher.

This Inner Teacher is known as the Holy Spirit. It is a part of God Himself whose purpose is to help you transcend the ego, to move beyond limitations, and to make decisions based on Love. The Holy Spirit is with you whenever you call on Him (or Her) for guidance. The Holy Spirit is never the first to speak, because this Voice is gentle, loving and quiet. So if you want to hear the advice of the Holy Spirit, you have to listen very carefully. The Voice is very quiet. But it is loving, knowledgeable and wise. Some people call it the still, small Voice inside.

You can access this Voice of Love whenever you want. This means you can always make a decision for Love. And when you do, and your INTENT is to be one with strength and Love and Light, then that is exactly where you will be. And your true nature, your Higher Self, will be in control – because you have made a decision based on Love. Each time you make such a decision it becomes easier. And you live more and more in the Light.

This is the whole purpose of your existence on earth, my Children – to learn to make decisions based not on the ego, but on Love; not on selfishness, but on sharing. Not on holding back, but on extending yourself.

This is probably the most important thing I have to share with you in this book.

As your Mother, I cannot tell you how important it is to choose Love throughout your entire life. As soon as you get this down and live it fully, you will be in Heaven, even if you are still on earth. Why continue to dwell in hell while on earth, living in fear, when you can make the choice for Heaven? You eventually will have to learn to make this decision, so why not sooner rather than later? It will make your life easier, and much more fun!

PRAYING WITH AN OPEN HEART

By praying with an open heart, I mean the opposite of praying out of fear, or praying from the standpoint of illusion. An authentic prayer comes from a heart that is humble, sincere, strong and clear. Sometimes this is the prayer of someone in great crisis. But it can also come from a Soul that is truly awake, alive to life, and in the giving mode. Such Souls are part of the Divine flow and the outreach and sharing of Love energy.

The opposite would be a prayer coming from a Soul that is sleeping, a Soul that is not open to new life experiences. I am speaking of a Soul more involved with selfish comforts and "taking" from the Divine system. Prayers from such a Soul do not carry the strength of clarity, nor the power of intent as does a prayer coming from, and centered in, the heart.

Many people are hypnotized into seeing life through the world's point of view. The collective ego can have a very strong pull and can be hard to break out of. I am here to help you see through new eyes.

THE POWER OF INTENT

When you pray, the key word is INTENT. Why are you praying? Your prayer may have many different intentions. Are you praying for Divine help? Are you praying to receive something? To obtain help in achieving something? Are you praying out of Joy? Are you praying out of a desire to link up with the collective brotherhood? Each of these instances has an intent. Be aware of the intent of your prayer.

Here is the reason: As a Child of God you have the ability to create. Prayer is not a passive process. Prayer is not simply your making a request to a higher power to grant you a mercy. Prayer is conscious intent and, thereby, creation.

When you have great clarity of intention, you will find it very powerful. Some people understand how to do this and they achieve wonderful things in their lives. They do this every day. And you can learn to pray in a similar way.

There is a difference between intention and intent. Intention is the general overall mindfulness of your prayer. It is more on the intellectual level.

Intent, on the other hand, comes from a feeling. It is attached to an emotion. It comes from the heart. And it has the power to move mountains. To have the ability to access your intent, then, means you have the ability to access your feelings and emotions. And then to link your feelings to your prayer. That is what puts power behind the prayer. And that power is your ability to create. Clear intent – linked with deep feeling –- and just about anything can be accomplished through this.

Another important aspect of this is authenticity. The prayer has to be authentic to the person praying. It has to be an appropriate extension of one's life. And the person praying has to have authenticity – or at least the desire to be authentic. You might think of this as something like sincerity. These aspects are more likely to come from a person who is truly awake. I do not mean awake to the ego life. I mean awake to a feeling of genuine Love, or connectedness.

These are elements of powerful prayer. When you have them placed in your heart you can literally create out of your own strength of alignment. I encourage you to think about these things. It is the destiny of each of my Children to learn how to pray powerfully. In my next message, or book, I will go deeper into the process of prayerful creation to show you more ways to expand your creative abilities.

EVERYONE IS HERE TO SERVE AND TO GIVE

The world, as I mentioned to you, has made much progress in *people-helping-people*. I feel a deep Joy in the kindness that I see playing out in millions of practical ways. But everyone is here to help. Not just some of us, not just those who conveniently have the time. Every Soul is here to serve his fellow man.

Giving, itself, is a kind of prayer. It involves a willingness to extend oneself on behalf of others. We refer to this as "serving." Serving implies nobility of intention – serving as a way of life, serving others as a privilege.

And everyone needs to give. People who are sick also need to reach out and give. People who are handicapped need to extend themselves on behalf of others. People who are financially hurting need to learn to give. Giving is a deep, important part of your life.

When giving gets to be too much of a tired habit, let yourself free and find a new way to reach out, so your outreach stays just that – a fresh way to give with an open heart.

Never make judgments about giving. You never really know the circumstances of another human being, or where a person might be stuck. Sometimes people are sick, or poor, or lost because of their inability to give. But sometimes this is not the case. Only the Holy Spirit really knows where a Soul is, as does Jesus Christ. It is never up to us to judge another. In fact, it is harmful to your Self to do so. Let judgments dissolve. That is the best way.

Sometimes people would like to give, but have forgotten how to give from their hearts. I am pointing this out so that those of you who may have forgotten about the importance of giving can think about this. If you feel stuck, always think: "Now, what can I give?" It always opens doors.

Giving is a celestial art. You can take it very high. It can take you all kinds of places. See giving as an opportunity for your own personal growth and outreach.

Part Four

Challenges of Nurturing

I HAVE BEEN SEEN OVER THE CENTURIES AS A SYMBOL OF MOTHER-hood. That is truly what my being is about. A mother is a nurturer. You should all see yourselves as nurturers. You are each here to nurture yourself – and one another. We nurture growth. We nurture Love. We nurture the forgiveness process. And we nurture the miracle, the way of seeing through the eyes of Christ.

There is the old way of seeing and the new way of seeing. The old way, which is still very much alive today, is the deceitful, selfish way. By this I mean the following: *Taking* (which ultimately means taking from yourself), *Fooling Others* (which means fooling yourself), and *Wasting Life* (which means wasting your own life). This is a sad and selfish way of living. It is the exact opposite of what my Son, Jesus Christ, came to teach. It is the inside-out way of living. This is the hard and difficult way to pursue life, because even though it may look like you're winning on the surface, in actuality your soul is losing ground.

The opposite of this is nurturing. Nurturing is a giving process. Nurturing is like tending a garden. It is a gentle process. Let us call it the Garden of the Heart. We water. We fertilize. We keep the weeds under control. If a weed creeps in overnight, we remove that weed soon the next day. The garden is continually watered and fertilized. The garden is loved, day by day. It is the energy we put into it, the energy of Love – consistent, caring Love – that builds the new energy, the new consciousness. That is what we mean by nurturing. It is a process of loving. I am a nurturer. You are a nurturer. And through nurturing, your miracle garden grows.

All Children should learn this process of loving and nurturing. They will learn that Love is a process that takes time and consistency. That is what creates the Garden of Nurturing Love.

Nurturing is a gentle, loving process. If we nurture day by day, Love grows. It is not any one act. It is a cumulative process of gentle loving over a period of time that produces a wonderful Garden of the Heart. As nurturers, we are cooperating with God the Father. He is the life energy of the garden itself. His energy makes it grow. As nurturers we tend the loving energy of our Father and create something. This is not just practical – it can be very beautiful.

When we speak about its opposite – the "Garden of Fear" we are talking about the old way of seeing life, the deceitful way. This is the opposite of the nurturing way. It is the way of "mis-tending," letting the weeds get out of control, ripping up the entire garden to get rid of the weeds and replacing them with something artificial that is supposed to look like a garden, but which will never, ever grow. This is not a process of nurturing. It is a process of soul death. It is a type of madness. It happens often in the world. It means making a cheap copy of the real thing – a copy that is supposed to substitute for the real thing. But of course this illusory ego imitation only breeds discontent.

In the Garden of Fear, I am referring to people who temporarily destroy their own lives and do not realize consciously that they are doing it. We see this happening sometimes when a person thinks that he or she has been mistreated. And rather than forgive and let go, that person decides to make an issue. And to make an issue, they cut off relations, go into anger and isolation, and cut off the Love that was in themselves. This is the antithesis of nurturing.

In such cases, the deceitful person stops tending his or her garden in partnership with God. The weeds appear. There is no watering. Bit by bit the garden withers and dies. With the deceitful person, something temporarily dies in the heart – the spark of Love moving through his or her life. This person temporarily chooses to end the partnership with God and decides to become his or her own god. It can happen slowly or quickly. This is always a story of separation.

This is also a scenario of fear. It is not Truth. Yet it happens often in the world. Deceitful people create problems for us in the world. No longer involved with nurturing and tending a garden of their own, they might start telling us how to grow our own garden. They might pretend that they have a garden when in actuality their garden is dead. They might try to pass a law saying that part of our garden belongs to them. In the dead seriousness of life, they might even start a war, which could destroy everyone's garden. There are many ways in which selfish souls who are no longer nurturing can become destructive to us. And that is one of the reasons I am reaching out to you through this message – to help you see what happens when people forget how to nurture. The "Garden of the Heart" is one of your most precious assets. Help your loved ones to see this. It is a gentle process, and it does not happen overnight. But its results can be extraordinary.

Nurturing was an important part of Jesus Christ's message. I, as His Mother, saw His message in terms of nurturing, and that is the message I bring to you today. I am asking you to become united with me in this. We must teach our Children how to nurture. We can teach our friends its value. And we must remember how to nurture ourselves.

ABOUT MOTHERING TODAY

We are now in an era where so many women make the choice to have Children later, to have fewer Children, and to do a superb job of raising each Child. The approach to mothering today is often one of quality rather than quantity. This is creating many wonderful results throughout the world – especially when the Children are given a strong spiritual foundation, and when they are not over-indulged materially. You will soon see the benefits and results of this style of mothering through the new spiritual and world leaders coming in the next few decades.

There are many Souls who are longing for the opportunity of a life on earth. Life on earth is a very precious opportunity for Soul development. Appreciate its significance. It represents a chance for Souls to be able to choose again – to choose Love rather than fear. When Love is consistently chosen over a lifetime, it strengthens the Soul and allows it to become imbued with Light and Grace.

Let me assure you that there are many millions of Souls longing for a chance, for the privilege, of living a life on earth. If you could only see the nobility and opportunity it is to be a Mother or a Father on earth, it would restructure your entire sense of values!

There were many outstanding Souls born to large families in the past centuries. With a family of 6 or 8 or 10 Children, each Child often did not have the kind of attention that a Child may have today. But when the principles of the family were in place there was always much opportunity to choose in favor of Love. And that is what life is all about. So many Souls received benefits from this. Today's earth families are much smaller. And, as a result, fewer Souls have the privilege of an earth life.

So be careful not to waste your precious lifetime on earth by being half-asleep to your spiritual growth, because that growth is the entire purpose of your life.

Choose to wake up! Choose to live for Love, to live for the outreach, for the giving, for the extension, for the outward stroke. Giving and receiving. This is the secret of life. This is true success. And its opposite – the inward stroke – taking and grasping, taking and withholding – the opposite – are what diminishes the Soul. Selfish energy, which is the direct opposite of giving, causes Souls to become weak and to waste their precious earth experience.

So always remember that life on earth is a great privilege for a Soul. That is why there is such great Joy at the birth of a Child. Each fabulous Soul – journeying to a human earth-life – has an important spiritual journey.

Each Soul takes so much loving and nurturing. But unless a Child is conceived in Love, carried to term in Love, born in Love and raised in Love, there is no sense in bringing another Child to earth to raise in fear.

Let me assure you that there is great rejoicing on the other side when a Soul returns after a life of Love! If you could see this, you would also rejoice at the ending of a life of a loved one after they have lived a life based on Love.

THE MOTHER-NURTURER

Because of my role as the Mother of Jesus Christ, I was called on to provide the female role that humans did not have in the male-conceived role of God the Father or in Jesus Christ. Few other women of my time were given major roles in life.

In time, my role expanded and I became Mother to millions. I have been honored through the centuries as the Madonna of great paintings, the "Notre Dame" of great cathedrals and universities. I was given a reverence for *what truly belongs to God.*

But the energy of this allows me to give with an enormously expanded capacity. And for this I have great gratitude and out of that gratitude, freedom and wonder. So I am a very joyous Soul. And I share this privilege with millions of other saints, Souls and angels throughout the universe. We field a tremendous amount of Divine Energy that is really…Love.

And all this is part of the Divine Plan for the *Undoing* and the *Coming Together.*

Many Catholics appreciate that I hold a place as a type of Divine Mother, Mother of Jesus Christ. But in essence I am not any more a part of the *Godship* than you are. We are all an extension of God's Divinity. And through the *Sonship*, or the Mystical Body of Jesus Christ, we join as an extension of the *Godship*.

And so I am needed as a Mother, as a nurturer. Any of you who need me, *come* to me – whether in tears or in Joy – because I am here to embrace you in gentleness and softness, and with all the nurturing that the female energy can provide.

But I am not the only comforter. Remember that the Divine Comforter is the Holy Spirit, who dwells within each of you. He is your Guide, your Inner Teacher. Listen for His quiet, gentle Voice of Truth within. He helps you to decide on your life lessons that will lead you to the full remembrance of who you are – a perfect Child of God.

The reason Catholics have a more developed knowledge of me is that they have focused on me, sometimes from childhood on. They have seen images of me in books. They have seen statues. They have been to devotions. They are better able to grasp the concept of a Blessed Mother, a female aspect of the Divine Sonship...And this is an important concept for my Children, whether they are Catholic or not. For a Child to have a spiritual mother to turn to in times of need, especially when their own mother cannot be there, is a valuable relationship.

It is a great advantage to both Children and adults in the world to remember that I can provide Grace whenever asked. I help to protect the innocence of Children. I help to surround each of my Children in Grace. Both of those functions are of great advantage in today's world.

CHILDREN AND DEPRESSION

The widespread depression and suicide experienced by your Children in this era is a very sad commentary on your culture and the world in which many of today's Children grow up.

Begin to be aware of how overexposed your Children are. Television brings them worlds of information that they have no need of. They grow up hearing and seeing thousands of television commercial messages that overload their young minds. They become aware of floods, earthquakes, plane crashes, robberies and killings all over the world. They hear about so many extraneous things they can do nothing about. This is very unnatural. This is cruel to inflict upon them. It awakens their compassion, but it creates an overload of quiet despair, a world of out control. Sensitive Children are easily burdened with this overload of scary and fearful information.

Children, from a very young age, also receive sexual innuendos from television. Their lives move much too fast in your electronic age.

And often parents "share" their emotional overload with their Children about marital or personal problems that the Child can do nothing about. Once again, it adds to an emotional overload on the part of my Children.

We must preserve the innocence and the mental sanity of our Children. If we can protect them from HALF of what the world pushes at them until they are ten or twelve years old...you would relieve an enormous amount of childhood depression!

Children need to have their consciousness protected from all the "noise" of the world. The human planet where you are is a very strange place in which to live. It is an insane place in many ways. So you will need to insulate your Children until they are old enough to cope with all the craziness of the world. You can create a safe world of sanity for your Children. In fact, it is quite necessary to do so. Because the way the system has evolved, it is often inhuman and builds all kinds of unnecessary pressures.

Children should not be pushed to compete, pushed to decide an occupation, or be otherwise "programmed" by their parents until they have had the time and space to grow up. You need to give Children their youth. Give them ten years at least to be Children. Try not to transfer all your problems onto their young shoulders too early. This may dwarf and overload them and limit their ability to serve later on in their lives. Nurture them first so they can be strong enough to move into the complex world of today.

The teen suicides you are seeing come from a sense of hopelessness, from living in a world that those Children see as confusing, out of control, and pointless. The more sensitive the Child, the harder it is to cope.

Think of the words PROTECTED ENVIRONMENT. Innocence has a great value and strength. Preserving innocence for Children will help create peacefulness. Be confident and know that you can create a controlled world of beauty, Light and Peace.

You do this by conscious decisions of what you want to shut out. Is it necessary to keep track of all local crimes? Turn off the television news. Visuals of crime make too deep an impact. Scan your news briefly – on the surface. Protect your consciousness. You will find that when you say no to the world, you begin to gain more power and control over your life.

Above all, remember that Children's minds are precious. They are like little blossoms. Protect their consciousness.

WORKING MOTHERS

A mother is a mother 24 hours a day. At the beginning, when your Children are very young, it is important to be near them. But do not feel deep guilt and remorse because you may have to work when your Children are very young. Remember that the Child is a Soul with a spiritual path all of its own. As our Children grow older it is up to us Mothers to let them progressively go so that they can fulfill their own spiritual destiny.

Throughout the centuries, since I was Mother to Jesus, some mothers have had the gift of having their Children very close to them through the first ten years. Others did not. The working mother is not a new phenomenon. Women have been going to the fields for centuries. Their Children did not always come with them, especially when the weather was inclement.

Mothers shared daytime responsibilities for raising Children. Thus, day care is not that new a concept.

If a mother has to work and put her Child in day care, she should not feel guilty about it. There are many advantages to day care. Children have the advantage of being with others. There is less separation in their lives. There is still time for intimacy with your Child. Being home all the time with your Child may not always be the perfect ideal.

There are other advantages for working mothers. Mothers and their Children do not get on each other's nerves as often. The mother can come home to her Child with a renewed spirit of mothering. It is a matter of Grace. If the working mother sees the blessings of her situation, then she lives in the Grace of that situation. Jesus was with both his father and me when growing up.

RAISING CHILDREN IN A SECULAR WORLD

The world has always been secular. The world has always offered opportunities to distract the mind from life's central issue – reunion in Love – so we can all return to Heaven.

The world you live in today is very distracting. There are so many places to go, so many things to buy. Entertainment is one of the biggest distractions, especially in the electronic age in which you live.

Your world can be a very hard place to teach Children a spiritual point of view. The television media can sometimes be a blessing. But it can sometimes be destructive to Children's minds. It is full of false images and illusions. It is the "golden calf" or idol of your times.

If I were a mother today I would be very, very careful of what images I allowed my Children to be exposed to. The mother and father's role is important not only as a nurturer, but as an example of love and discipline. This is one of the privileges of being a parent. Be careful of the young consciousness of each of your Children. Be careful of their friends as they start growing up because it is difficult to keep their minds clear if their friends have confused minds.

Clarity of mind is an extremely important gift you can give your Children. This means that you, too, need to keep your mind somewhat free of all the chatter of today's world. You can do this by being more simple and serene, rather than complex and overly busy.

The mark of a great Soul is its simplicity and clarity. That is one of the greatest things about my Son, Jesus Christ. He had great focus and clarity as to what He was about. It was His clarity, focus and concentration that enabled Him to perform miracles. He would have made a great father on earth.

If your Children do not have a father, teach them to look to Jesus Christ as a father. I assure you that God the Father will be pleased. Closeness to Jesus Christ is a very strengthening force for Children – as well as adults.

SPIRITUAL EDUCATION FOR CHILDREN

Spiritual education is very important for your Children. If it is of high regard in *your* value system, so it may be also for *them*. You, as parents, have a certain power to transfer values to them. Teach them to pray from the time that they are very young. Pray with them. Take them to church. Teach them to nurture. Become their spiritual teacher by living Love.

You can inspire faith in your young ones when you are able. Other young ones may be impossible to get through to. Do not worry if your Child seems to be in another world. Each represents a Soul on its individual path. Some Children are truly in another place and they will seem to have no relationship to your consciousness. At times you may even wonder if it is your Child. Nurture them nonetheless. Each is a perfect Child of God in his or her own way. Some of our Children simply require more patience than others do.

Try not to inundate your Children with spiritual matters and religion.

That could cause them to close their hearts to spiritual growth. Be subtle...build an interest. Take them to church. Live with reverence. Say grace at meals. Do bedtime prayers with them. Try to keep their innocence intact. Nurture their love of the spiritual and your spirituality will also grow.

Young Children are not so far removed from Heaven. They remember God better than you do. Children have a very mystical side to them. And always remember that they are your teachers, too. Be open to receiving gifts of wisdom from your Children.

Be very careful about being judgmental about religion, church or spiritual growth. Never criticize religion in front of young Children. The world's cynicism will get to them soon enough. I am not talking about trying to turn your Children into little saints; but try to keep an element of sacredness in your family's life. With it, your Children will be much stronger as they go through life.

ABOUT ABORTION

My Children, abortion is one of those extremely sensitive areas – because *everything* about the topic is very sensitive. The child. The mother. The father. The integrity. The Light. The promise. The life situation. And so I will begin this discussion with a very high level of sensitivity which I hope will set your own tone of sensitivity and non-judgment with regard to abortion.

I do not advocate abortion because it is such an unnatural act. It is a painful process – spiritually, mentally, emotionally, and physically.

However, just because a girl is able to conceive does not mean that she is capable of becoming a mother. Motherhood is a privilege that requires emotional maturity, the ability to Love, to be resourceful and responsible. If a prospective mother has not achieved this maturity, she may not be ready for motherhood.

Sometimes, life's current circumstances simply do not allow for motherhood. Then one must decide with the Holy Spirit what is right, and then act from the heart. This is often a very painful process for a prospective mother to go through and takes great courage.

It makes me very sad to see a mother forced to grow her fetus in a womb where there is not Love, but fear. Mothering is a privilege, and only women in a loving state of mind should go through the process of bringing a Child into the world. It is not kind nor loving to bring a Child of God into a home of fear, lack and limitation. Thus, to force a woman to carry a Child she is not prepared to Love and nurture is not in harmony with God's law of Love.

It takes a great deal of Love, balance, emotional maturity, energy and stability to raise a single Child of God. It also takes resources and the support of others, beyond the mother. Raising a child alone is an enormous responsibility. One must never assume or judge that another individual has all those qualities. Having and raising a child is a huge commitment. Let us never forget that, nor take it lightly.

As your Blessed Mother I cannot give you a blanket yes or no on any aspect of abortion because the issue is so deeply personal – and it is really between you and the Holy Spirit. One must always do what is right according to the circumstances of your life, and the circumstances of your heart.

You are here on earth to make decisions. You are either making decisions based on Love, or you are making decisions based on fear. This applies to every aspect of your life. And it applies to abortion as well. Decisions based on Love are the only decisions to make.

Each of you has an Inner Guide whom we shall call the Holy Spirit. It is your Inner Voice of Light and Truth. The Holy Spirit is always there, if you call upon Him, He can help you make the right decision in every circumstance. In light of this, you are never alone. You always have an inner Wisdom that you can depend upon.

It is extremely important that you consider any aspect of abortion with the Holy Spirit. He will help you know what is right for you. What is right for you depends upon the individual circumstances of your life, coupled with what you know is right in your heart, and how you can handle the responsibilities of motherhood. Each circumstance of Love is individual.

Thus, there is never a blanket answer as to what is right for you, because what is right for you is between you and the Holy Spirit. This is a very intimate area. That is why there can be no judgment about abortion, because no one may judge Holy Spirit's inner wisdom. No one may tell the Holy Spirit what to do. And no one may judge a decision made with the Holy Spirit in Love. This area is both sacrosanct and intimate.

When decisions are made with the Holy Spirit they will have an inner Wisdom. And with those decisions there is a sacred trust that relates to Inner Truth, and no one may judge that Inner Truth.

This is the pivotal point regarding abortion, and everything radiates out from that point of Truth. If it is right to have a baby, it will be known from the Holy Spirit according to the life path laid out with the Holy Spirit. All decisions of life experiences are made with Him – from the learning experiences you will have at each level of life – to your very death. Each life experience is the perfect lesson for you to learn. Life is not a random game. There is a learning plan laid out for your life. And how you choose to play out that plan is up to you. The idea is to play each circumstance with Love.

So let no one be a judge of abortion in any way. It is much too intimate an issue. It is extremely difficult on the mother and the father because these are most tender questions. Remember that the answer *always* lies with the Holy Spirit. And so there should be no embroiling emotions around this topic. The challenge to each of you, the challenge of your learning experience, is to go within and let Light lead the way. For if you judge another, you are judging yourself. If you consistently judge others you are consistently judging yourself. And if you keep judging yourself you will weigh yourself down to the point where your life may become very oppressive and complicated on several levels simultaneously.

If you pretend that you know all the answers of life, according to some notion in your mind, then you are out of touch with the Holy Spirit. And it is your duty and responsibility to get back in touch with Him. And when you do, He will guide you as to how to start making your inner decisions based on Love.

As your Blessed Mother, I, too, am subject to the inner wisdom of the Holy Spirit. For He is God's very extension. He is the Inner Teacher for each of us. Allow me to assure you that everything I do is in alignment with the Holy Spirit. I still consult Him on many issues. And so should you.

Let there be no guilt surrounding abortion. Guilt is not the province of the Holy Spirit. The Holy Spirit is about Love and freedom. Let all other issues surrounding abortion be considered in His Light and Love. If you find your emotions flaring up, always remember to let go and choose Love . For peace is your natural state and peace requires detachment.

WHEN INNOCENT YOUTHS DIE

My Children, I know it is hard for you to fathom the death of a young Child. Perhaps you see this as vengeance or as a great mystery. Why would God take an innocent Child or a youth out of his or her life when they have not fully had a chance to live life? Let me help you understand it in this way.

In the first place, God the Father is not directly involved in the day-to-day or year-to-year running of the world. I hope this is not upsetting to you. We are not His puppets. He has given each of us Free Will, which is an awesome responsibility. The world is your game, not God's. You bear ultimate responsibility for what happens here. So blaming God is not in order.

In the second place, God is perfect, pure Love while the world is an error state. The two simply do not equate. God is perfect. Human beings on earth are in a dream state of their own making.

God is not up in the Heavens, making decisions, pressing buttons, pulling strings, and controlling your life. He is not evening things up. He is not judging, choosing, deciding your fate.

God is God. He is Absolute Love. No more need be said. He is not involved in the day-to-day running of your universe. That would be a disturbing responsibility for a being *Who Is Pure Love.*

So why do young people sometimes die if God isn't calling them?

Because they have reached a level of completion and they are ready to move on.

To grasp this better, I must first explain to you that God the Father sent you the Holy Spirit to help you work your way out of this error state. That is why the Holy Spirit is here to help you with the "Undoing," as I call it. Other helpers include my Son, Jesus Christ, and myself, Mary, your Mother of Grace. The major contingent of Helpers also includes the angels and saints of God who are with us. It is part of their mission to assist. I was a human once. So was Jesus. So were all the saints. We are still part of the network that helps you.

When you see a Child or a teen or a young person die in the prime of life, the first thing I would say to you is refrain from any judgment. None of us knows anything about the personal relationship another Soul has with the Holy Spirit and his or her life lesson.

Each person has his or her own path, I assure you. No two paths are alike, just as no two Souls are ever quite alike. Each Soul is a SPECIAL creation of God. And each individual Soul has its own path. Some people are here to live and to love in a short period of time. They have very little work to finish up before leaving to become part of the "support team," so to speak. Others are here for a longer duration.

So if one person has five years to finish up on the planet, and another ten years or twenty years – or eighty years – what is the difference? In our realm, with no time, there is no difference at all.

In your realm on earth, however, how much time you have is of great, great importance. That is because you are not certain of your connection to the Divine, and you sometimes fear the worst.

When you lose someone in their prime, be assured that they are simply "moving on" or "up" to the next level.

Be assured that they are Love, that they are safe, and that no Soul ever "dies." You will all stay in circulation after death, and you will be reunited with particular Souls again after death, if you so wish. Free Will always stays an important part of your matrix.

There is no such thing as death – as you may picture it. No one dies and is plunged into everlasting darkness. People may plunge themselves into a temporary darkness of their own choosing, their own personal hell that they have created. But it is only temporary – until they choose again. Eventually they have to come back and face the Light.

So rather than calling it DEATH, think of it as a TRANSITION. It is merely a change between levels of being.

A baby or Child who dies early may just have a short mission to live out – some small unfinished forgiveness to undo. Perhaps it is a learning experience for the parents or the family, to help them learn to let go and trust. It is all part of a plan, a Divine plan. But not a plan that God devises for us. Rather, it is a plan that we, in our free, unconscious will decide upon with the Holy Spirit. We all have our particular life missions, however obscure they may be. Live your lives with the assurance that you are not a leaf adrift in the wind. You are part of a beautiful, complex program that you have had a hand in designing for yourself. Think of it as a rich woven tapestry. And everyone's story is integrated into a part of this magnificent tapestry. It is part of the gloriousness of creation, of which you are an important, active part.

GUNS AND CHILDREN

I am very proud of mothers and fathers who take a stand against weapons. If we love our Children, we protect them. And that means keeping them away from firearms. That means that guns should not be given to your Children as toys with which they can play-act. That means that we should not use guns on entertainment shows and give the appearance that guns do not really hurt. Children need to understand that guns are a serious matter. They need to be taught a deep awareness of the significant danger of guns. Children must understand clearly that guns are not toys, but that guns kill.

We should teach our Children, rather, that true courage is to live without guns. Guns are used for hiding behind. Guns have nothing to do with Love. Guns are fear-based. They are based on defense. They are based on attack. They are based on aggression, and on a false sense of protection.

Please teach your Children that true courage is living without guns. Love is protection enough.

Instead, teach them to call on me for defense. Call on Christ or the Holy Spirit. Do that often, and you and your Children will find yourself in a safe space where guns are completely unnecessary.

There is an old saying: *Live by the sword, die by the sword.* Today's version could be: *Live by the gun, die by the gun.* It is your choice. I ask you to move beyond the fear of needing to have a gun. It is a primitive way of being. Thank you, mothers, for your devotion in this area.

CHILDREN LOST ON DRUGS

Love your Children lost on drugs. Be there to love them and support them. They need nurturing of the Soul to heal. See past their limitation to the perfect Children of God they are. Be a mirror to them, a mirror of Light. That is what they need most.

But do it silently and firmly. Never preach. Be with them as a silent, loving strength. Express to them how much you care that they be free again. They need to hear that someone outside them cares, really cares. If no one cares, they feel lost.

Care. Pray. Call on me. Together we will surround them silently with Grace. And in time, if their Free Will is ready, they will make a decision to move toward the Light. But that is a decision they must make in their own hearts.

You cannot threaten or use fear tactics. Love is simply the only answer. And it may take time. Each Soul is in a period of transition. Each Soul has its own path. That is why the Holy Spirit works with each of you quietly and gently, to lead you out of the labyrinth of your fears. It is a very delicate process.

Your Heavenly Father gave this specific function to the Holy Spirit many eons ago, the moment you removed yourself from paradise. He will be with you, directing each of you, until you are "undone" of fear and ready to return to the Light from which you came.

THE SUFFERING OF MOTHERS AND CHILDREN

Love those mothers and Children who are in poverty and who are suffering due to injustices of the world's economic system. Help them. Love them. Practice giving to them – rather than ignoring them. They need help. Often they need food, resources, and time. They are often very overworked. The selfishness of the economic system seldom concentrates on the needs of my Children and mothers at the base level of society.

You can reach out to them. There is no need for poverty in the rich world you have created. There is great need for sharing, however. The *people helping people* movement has taken care of some of these mothers and Children in poverty. Many more need help. Those of you who have lost Children, or who did not have Children, or have grown Children – perhaps you could take on someone else – to help and nurture them. See past their trials to the perfect, loving, innocent Children of God they are.

When you provide a mirror of perfection to each other, both can react to that perfection and BE the perfect Children of God that you ARE.

Seeing past the illusions of this world, the illusions that limit us, is to see your true selves. See these lovely people as yourselves. Look into their eyes and see the Light of Christ. There is a Oneness that transcends all limitations. As you reach out to help your brothers and sisters, you will experience a mystical joining that will give great meaning to your lives. See this service as an opportunity.

INJUSTICES TOWARD MEN

So many men are suffering today because of the way the legal system has taken their families away. They are hurting because life has not been easy for them. Many have become jobless, estranged, and embittered.

The economic system does not work for many men in today's world. There are many in fear, men who feel they are victims of the system. They, too, need help and prayers. See them, too, as the perfect Children of God that they are.

TERRORISM IN TODAY'S WORLD

My Children, my heart is overwhelmed with sorrow at the cruel acts of terrorism that have hurt so many of my innocent sons and daughters across the world. Terrorism is one of the saddest chapters of modern human evolution. The planned destruction of other innocent souls is so heartless, so insane, so soul-wrenching, that it hurts me and my Son very, very deeply.

This senseless hate is an impediment to the forward motion of the loving world. It often stems from old, segmented fear and hatefulness that has chosen not to evolve along with the rest of humanity.

Please be careful in how you meet this challenge. To retaliate with vengeance will only unleash the old "eye for an eye, tooth for a tooth" ancient energies on both sides. I know that you have grown far beyond those old ways in today's world evolution. I pray that wisdom will prevail and that today's leaders will find sophisticated, expedient, and wise ways of containing and dissolving hostile terrorism throughout the world.

In addition to the worldly ways of containing this violence, let me remind you that there is great power in the critical mass of prayer. In your prayers you can powerfully focus on dissolving terrorism and its senseless acts. Remember that your prayer must come from your Love within, not from any form of personal hatred. You must not fall into a similar mindset of fear. Pray with Love that these old, hostile energies be dissolved off the face of your planet.

The intention and power of your prayer can be very effective to weaken terrorism, its focus, its planning, so that it dissipates and dissolves back into the nothingness of the dark side of eternity. Remember that praying together in unison creates a critical mass of energy, which can be extremely effective.

Be comforted that there are always side benefits that come forth from these mishaps. The injustices of terrorism cause many souls to wake up, reshape their priorities, redirect their thinking and lead greater lives, of more depth, as a result of these atrocities. Meanwhile, remember that I am always there to comfort those who have been victimized by these assaults, on both sides of the veil. Ask for my help, and I am with you, or your lost friend.

Part Five

Caught Between Fear & Love

PEOPLE PRAY TO ME...WOULD I BE SO KIND...WOULD I PLEASE HEAL the cancer, the AIDS, the Alzheimer's, heal all sickness and disease in this world? It is not my province to interfere that way. Whatever a Soul decides to experience, be it an illness or a death, that is a decision that is made out of his or her own Free Will. Some people choose to discipline themselves through illness and pain because no one ever taught them that they had the chance to learn through Love and Joy. And so they are only capable of learning through a painful experience. I am not here as your Mother to "kiss your hurts" so they will all go away and everything will be perfect for you. You are working through your lessons with the Holy Spirit whether you are aware of it or not. Subconsciously you and the Holy Spirit decided on a curriculum and you will always have the final say as to what it will be. Unfortunately, many of you do not know that you need not suffer pain to learn your lessons.

I am a Mother sent here to help and nurture you – to help you understand how to choose Love. This way you can stand on your own two feet as a Child of God, realize your perfection, and heal the limitations you think you have. There are many ways that you choose to become whole again, and each of them is a learning experience of your choosing.

You may choose to experience Heaven on earth, and to learn through Love to get to that place. It is part of your journey of spiritual evolution to choose that destination and arrive there.

I am here to save you a thousand years from your journey if you will listen to me and attain the discipline to think in new ways. If I cured AIDS, humans would simply invent some new disease. People use the vehicle of diseases for learning. You see, man often loves suffering. It helps him to overcome his guilt. And he does have the Free Will to do this.

However, there is no need for guilt. For how can a perfect Soul, perfectly created by God the Father, ever come to imperfection? Any time that any one of my Children makes a mistake he or she need merely to choose again. God is perfectly forgiving.

Even if you have made a mistake and wandered off into darkness, simply choose again. Choose Love, and come back into the Light. Never focus on what you are not. That is a disservice to your Heavenly Father who is Great. You are Great also. You are created by Him in His image. Rejoice and respect this fact.

Human ignorance also invented cancer. It is a very slow way of death for people who feel stuck and need to move on. Its advantage is that it often gives a Soul time to get its affairs in order and prepare for the process of dying. But, you see, neither suffering nor sickness is necessary at all. It is just part of the mass hypnosis on the earth.

When a person is ready to die, to pass on in life, that person can choose to die quietly during sleep or while sitting quietly reading a book. Primitive man, when ready to die, often would just wander off into the woods and lie down. Death would come quietly, with dignity. Death is simply a passing from one plane to another. So do not think that sickness need necessarily precede death. Remember that you always have the Free Will to choose again and thereby simplify the process of passing on.

LONG, DRAWN-OUT ILLNESSES

Modern medicine, the way you know it, has many very scientific and creative ways of assisting and helping out human beings. Let me assure you that many of these processes were created in a loving way to help other Souls with their pain.

Always remember, you are free to choose your own path. If you are ready to die, you should be able to die quietly and with dignity, just as I mentioned that primitive man did. That is your right as a Child of God.

The same applies to the area of mercy killings. Should the state have the right to deprive you of your right to die? You are a Child of God. This gives you the privilege and the responsibility to make personal decisions for yourself. You do not need legislation to direct your own Soul choices. This is an area for your own Free Will.

When death is near and there is little possibility of recovery, remember that there is no reward for suffering indefinitely. Suffering is not something that God wants for you. In such a case, you are free to make the decision to free yourself to the next level.

Each person has the power to decide about his or her own death. It is not unusual to hear people say: "God called him," or "God took her back." These ideas of God calling someone home removes the personal responsibility from the decision to die. Some people must have an excuse like that to shift the responsibility away from Self. People either will to live, or they will to die. Death is a decision made by an individual Soul, along with the Holy Spirit. The decision is made subconsciously. Death is not as accidental as it may seem. Understand this and you will not feel like a victim. Understand this and it will free you from your fear of death.

And please remember, it takes personal responsibility to decide to die. People know when their life and purpose are lived out. Try not to hold onto them if it is their time to go.

The basic fact is that all humans have to pass on from human life at some point. Either we have learned all of our lessons and are through, or we are in need of new lessons and experiences to evolve.

Remember, however, that there is no real death, as in a finite ending. A Soul never dies. It only goes through a transition between levels. If you can accept it that way, it can become less emotional and less fearful.

MIRACULOUS CURES AND CHRONIC ILLNESS

Each time there is a "miraculous cure" it is the purity of intention of your heart – a Love spark that is the real initiator of the miracle. I only provide the Grace. Your Free Will makes the true decision for healing.

The answer is always the same. It is all in your way of seeing. Weren't there many truly sick people healed by my Son Jesus? Yes, there were. Are there not "truly sick" people healed every day? Indeed there are.

And what does "incurable" mean? Is it not possible to cure even the meanest infection, the most malignant tumor? Of course it is possible. So nothing is incurable. You are not your body. Your body is merely an instrument of communication to serve you while you are here on earth. When you leave earth, you leave your body behind. Most find this quite a blessing. It is a joy to be Light and without a body, let me assure you.

So, can you look beyond the illness, through the sickness and see the Soul as the Perfect Child of God that it is? Then you will not be deceived by fear. You will see the Truth that your Heavenly Father sees. He sees each of you as perfect, the way He created you.

And so does my Son, Jesus Christ. He sees your perfection too, as do I. You should begin to see your brothers and sisters this way, as perfect Children of God. That is the only lasting reality. See past any surface sickness. See past all imperfections. See past any errors that a Child of God may have temporarily chosen. See past all the illusions. See the real Child of God. My Children, you often use sickness for many different purposes. The self-deception of the circumstance is that you often picture yourself as a "victim" of the sickness.

In Truth, my Children often endure sickness for their own learning experience. Many human Souls are resigned to suffering as part of their life process. And of course, sickness brings its own rewards – sympathy, time out, attention. This is played out, not on a conscious level, but on a subconscious level where there may be a hidden agenda and subversive will. Most people do not realize that sickness is a hard game to play, with penalties. But it is the principal way that some people choose to learn.

It is truly amazing how many Souls there are who patiently accommodate the sick rituals that other Souls live out. Have you ever heard the caretaker of an sick person saying: "I'm too busy to get sick. I have too many things to take care of." Have you noticed how people who voice these words often keep themselves in good health so that they can carry on to serve someone else? People of this mindset often do not get sick – because they do not give themselves permission to take on illnesses. This is a case where virtue is its own reward.

LIFE-THREATENING ILLNESSES

People have great creative powers. When someone decides subconsciously that it is time for them to pass away – there are several acceptable ways of bowing out of life. An easy way is to decide to slip away in sleep. No suffering is necessary. There are many options. It is important to realize that God is not sitting up in Heaven, planning fatal illnesses for certain people, such as: "You will have a tumor of the brain...You will have lung cancer..." God the Father is removed in a cosmos of Perfect Peace and Love. He is not involved with error

– certainly not the error of assigning illnesses to people. People choose their own illnesses subconsciously out of their own misguided creativity. Sometimes humans have old patterns of fear woven into their thinking. This is due to lack of awareness of spiritual law. This is hard to tell a person with an incurable disease, but Souls often end their life in a way consistent with the amount of time they need to wrap up their life gracefully.

Part of the hypnosis and illusion of this world is that people have confused and misguided ideas about illness. They may think that they are predisposed to cancer, heart disease, strokes or arthritis. And if that is what they believe, it is what will occur. Thus anyone who wishes to believe in predisposition toward a particular illness may do so. And the illness will work for them exactly – as precisely as they want it to. Humans attract exactly what they fear, if they dwell on it long enough. They also attract exactly what they Love, if Love is their focus.

However, if you decide that your father's heart problem was *his* heart problem, you may leave it at that, and not carry the guilty idea of a genetic weakness into the next generation. You then give yourself freedom from such worries and fears. I give you permission to lay those old fears to rest. I tell you, the era is coming when people will become more enlightened and tired of the idea of disease. They will recognize that they have the power to be well whenever they choose. They will grasp the idea that sickness is unnecessary. They will not feel the fear of the illness and then subsequently attract what they fear.

And when that occurs, health care industries around the world will focus on wellness. Wellness is the new thought pattern toward which you should all be heading. When this becomes more widespread in this new millennium, your doctors and health care professionals will take on an entirely new role. They will turn their energies away from surgery, from drugs, from medical fixing…to a new era of optimum health. They will find many new, creative ways to help you feel your best, to assist you in looking wonderful, and helping you to enjoy life in your healthy body well into your 100s. Health care will reach new heights of respect and joyousness, and you will all benefit by feeling wonderful most of the time. This is in the future. In the meantime, if you do not want to be sick, do not be sick. There is no God to appease with your sickness. There is no sacrifice necessary to gain another "pearl in your crown."

The entire idea of sacrifice is a very old and primitive idea. Sacrifice was used out of fear to appease a vengeful God. Let me assure you, our God is a God of Love. The last thing He would ever want to do is to punish one of His Children. He Loves you all. He is waiting for your return. He wants you to be perfectly safe and happy at all times. He wants the best for you.

So you have to want the best for yourself, too. The basic rationale you can have for sickness is that you chose it for your learning in conjunction with the Holy Spirit. And, in that case, it is easier to see the value in the discipline of sickness. But remember, that you *chose* the sickness on a subconscious level, with the Holy Spirit as a part of your spiritual journey through life. It was chosen as a lesson, to help you learn to love. It was not thrust upon you, because you unquestionably have Free Will. A sickness can open you up to many valuable new life experiences. If you see it that way, it will be closer to the Truth.

ABOUT DEATH AND DYING

Most Souls are not prepared enough to "ascend," so to speak, to the fullness of God and to the highest plane of Heaven at death. My Son, Jesus Christ, did. But He was one of the most extraordinary Souls who ever lived on earth. He is a prototype for each of you. He is a prototype for me. He truly ascended and rejoined with the Father. But the important thought to keep in mind is that He still has a mission with us all.

For all Souls there is a continuance of the learning process after death. Many Souls still have to reach the decision for Love and the decision for Heaven. Each of you must choose in your own heart.

You will continue learning with the Holy Spirit after death. It will go on and on until you finally reach the realization that, indeed, you are Love and that you make all decisions based on Love, for Love is what you are.

After you reach that point, then you will eventually make the decision for Heaven. At that point, you are in Heaven. Not the ultimate Heaven on the highest plane where God the Father is…That will come later when all Souls are ready to go back to God as a unified Whole, in Oneness. This will be the Second Coming that I have spoken of. Instead, it is a Heaven where you join with others to assist other Souls still on the path.

RETURNING AS A WHOLE

One rather jarring note to the fact of our spiritual evolution is that we will all return to God the Father as a Whole. So there is no need for anyone to rush up to the front of the line. Help all of your brothers with their lessons of Love. That way you will actually be helping yourself. Remember, there is really only One of us. Take time to help your brothers who are in prison or who are under-privileged. They are part of you. We will all arrive at the Godhead in unity.

Because of the relationship that each of you has with the Holy Spirit, never assume that you know what is best for another human being. You never know another's lesson plan for the Undoing. And it is not up to you to change a brother or a sister. There needs to be much respect for the evolvement of a human Soul. It is a very sacred process. Each Soul has its own individual path, so do not compare. Respect each person's uniqueness. Respect your own.

THE "UNDOING" PROCESS

One of the main purposes of your life is forgiveness. I am not speaking of forgiveness in the old sense of forgiveness where you magnanimously decide to "forgive" someone out of the goodness of your heart. I am speaking about something different.

The process of forgiveness through the Holy Spirit is like the peeling of an onion, layer by layer, until you get to the very heart of the onion which means you are back to your Soul essence, free and clear.

The peeling, in your case, is the shedding of your old way of looking at life. I am speaking of the ideas that keep you separated, the things that keep you upset. Layer after layer you let these things go. Your tensions and anxieties are embodied between these layers. As part of the Undoing you let go of past disappointments, past judgments of others, and judgments you hold about yourself. You also let go of past anger and injustice. As you let go and "forgive" these layers, you free yourself to be more of who you really are. This is the "Undoing" process.

As some souls laughingly say, "Forgiveness is giving up all hope of a better past." What is past is over. It cannot be changed. And so you must re-create your life anew in each "Present Moment." The Present Moment is really all you have. It is where you have your power of choice and Free Will.

While it may be theoretically possible to accomplish the Undoing in a heartbeat, no one does it that way. Even Jesus Christ had His process. For most people the process takes many years...it takes lifetimes. Keep in mind that it is THE main purpose of your life. It is why you are here on earth. So please, do not waste your time pondering the purpose of your existence. THIS IS IT! Forgiveness and the Undoing.

Some accomplish very little of the Undoing during their lifetime. But everyone must accomplish it sometime before they enter the Kingdom of Heaven. So, the sooner the better. "Unless you become like a little Child you cannot enter the Kingdom of Heaven." My Son's words – relate precisely to just this.

It is not an option for Souls to decide whether or not they want to go through the Undoing. Everyone must do it eventually. You simply have the freedom to decide on the time you want to do it. You can delay it and keep yourself in pain as long as possible. Or you can choose Love and Heaven sooner and come to inner Peace earlier on your path.

People who delay this decision are like the last stragglers onto an airplane flight. They hold up everyone else. But, in Truth, the ultimate "plane back to

Heaven" does not leave until every last Soul is aboard. All of us must have our egos undone in order to get back to the innocence of being a Child. It is a matter of time and Love. Unless you are like a Child (of God) you cannot enter the Kingdom of Heaven.

For this to happen, every last one of our rebellious Children will need to be undone – every addict, every hardened criminal, every lost Soul. So we cannot just lock up our brothers and throw away the key. We must undertake joint responsibility for teaching Love to each and every Soul.

In the long run, we will have to gather each Soul, just like a shepherd gathers the lost sheep. That is why I am here to teach you about nurturing. It is the same message my Son gave. Truth never changes. Angels are helping Souls in the direction of Love at every moment. So will you someday.

ABOUT HELL

Yes, my Children, there is such a thing as hell, but only the hell that individual Souls create for themselves. Many of the people you pass in your cars every day are in personal hells of their own creation. Hell is a state of mind. Hell is a state of mind where there is no hope, no forgiveness – of others or of oneself. It is a very mean, claustrophobic, cynical, trapped way of seeing life.

Hell is judgment of others, which means the very same judgment of oneself. It is separation – self-imposed, terrible, narrow, and tight thinking. Many people on earth live in hell, I assure you. It is a spiritual law that when you judge others, you also judge your inner Self in like measure.

People who are in their own personal hell will have to eventually let go of their darkness and return to the Light. They have to re-create their own world. No one can release you from your personal hell. You have to do it for yourself. We can give others Love and understanding. We can give them freedom of judgment by having no opinion about where they are. But ultimately everyone must decide against their personal hell.

However, I am happy to tell you that NO – there is no hell with fire and a devil and everlasting suffering. You have the power to create that type of hell in your imagination, of course. But no – no such place as hell exists. Hell has been used as a threat for millenniums to keep people in line, to keep them in fear of the afterlife. But the real hell is a mental state of mind. Those who choose hell in their own minds may seem like dangerous people, but they are really just Souls in need of loving. They fear just retribution from a judgmental God. And of course, no such mean God exists, except in your own mind.

God is Absolute Beauty and Love. He is unaware of your error. He knows only Love. He is centered in a place of Perfect Peace and Perfect Love. He waits for you to wake up from your earthly dream and rejoin Him. But you must do it of your own Free Will. Perhaps it would be more accurate to say that we have removed ourselves from His perfection temporarily, but that eventually we will all return to our natural state with Him.

Always remember that you are safe within the loving arms of the Holy Spirit, Jesus Christ, God the Father, as well as with all your brothers and sisters. And of course there is me, your Mother of Grace, your Mother of Miracles. A truly Loving God who is made of Love would never choose anything mean or punishing for His Children, His offspring made in His own image.

So I tell you now — I tell you with great honesty — you have nothing to fear. You have nothing but happiness, joy, good health, spiritual wealth and well-being to look forward to. If you choose to learn to Love, your life will improve. The more and more you learn to forgive and let go, the better your life will become. All your emptiness, all the things in your life that do not work, will be replaced by Love.

THERE IS NOTHING TO FEAR

There is nothing to fear. There is nothing to worry about. I am with you. You are safe. When you fully realize this you can relax under the mantle of my Grace. Think of my energy as a beautiful, protecting layer of Love that surrounds you. It is a gift. When you can accept the idea of my gift, it is yours.

I am here for your happiness at all times. All you have to do is focus on me. Hold in mind the image of me as Your Mother of Grace. Look at the new image of me that I have given you. Hold it in your heart, and you will feel my presence at the very core of your being.

I am a "good news" Mother of Grace. Some of my Children already have too much bad news surrounding them. I am here to help relieve them of that pain.

The voice of fear is all around you, but you must learn to ignore it. There is fear on the news, so you have to learn to insulate yourself. You cannot waste your energy by buying into fear all the time. Choose again. Choose Peace. Choose Love. Choose me. I am much better than fear.

Love is basically all there is on the plane where I am. Love is ultimately all there is for you and all the Sonship. But you are not entirely sure of it. So you play around with the word Love. It has many different meanings for you. Love is very ELUSIVE to most people on earth. This is Love with a large "L" because it is the ultimate fact of your existence. Please remember to teach only Love, for Love is what you are.

This is Truth for you, even if you do not fully understand what it means for you at this time. This is mysticism. Live with mysticism. Live with the idea that you do not understand everything wonderful that is happening to you now. Live with trust in the life process. Trust is an ingredient of Love. Trust the softness of life, the beauty, the ease that should come naturally to you as a Child of God. Trust, and it will come to surround you. It feels good and it is your gift.

Love brings pleasure – a desirable state. Pleasurable states should be desired by everyone. Yet many Souls are afraid to enjoy pleasure, so they push it away. It is because deep in their hearts they feel that they are not worthy of pleasure, not good enough to enjoy it.

The idea of sin and unworthiness is deeply embedded in your Souls and this must be undone and changed to Love. Otherwise, you will attract only fear and dis-ease. On the other hand, when your energy is going in the direction of Love, you have the power to draw to you the beauty, the ease, and the pleasure of the world. Along with this comes the spirit of accomplishment and creativity that springs from living life on the inside.

You can achieve your own Heaven consciousness here on earth. Many people here are enjoying their Heaven-on-Earth as we speak. I encourage you to create your own Heaven, based on Love. I will have more to share with you about this in the years to come. This first book from me is more to re-orient your thinking to new concepts. In my next book I will share with you more details about how to accomplish this in your daily life.

YOU ARE NOT A VICTIM OF THE WORLD

You are not a victim of the world, unless you see yourself as a victim and act as a victim. As a Child of God you have great latitude as to the decisions you make in life, and how you react to the world around you. React with Love. You are here on earth to learn to choose Love. You are here to learn to choose Love 100-200-300 times a day. You do this by the way your live your entire day.

When you awaken, you can choose to wake with Love – Love for yourself – being part of the Sonship that you are. (I do not want to seem male-oriented. When I use the word Sonship it includes daughters as well as children, as well as the elderly, as well as sons of God. It is an embracing term. It implies the complete Wholeness of all Souls in the universe. It is a term of great Love and endearment. Please understand it that way.)

CHOOSING LOVE VS. CHOOSING FEAR

Fear is confusion. Fear is tightness. Fear is being lost. Fear is separation. Fear is the instroke. Fear is taking. Fear is the opposite of outstroke, reaching out. Fear is withdrawal and contracting inward. Fear makes us brittle and constricted.

Fear produces what you call "anxiety" or "stress." It is a defeatist way of thinking. It has been the accepted mode on the planet earth for many eons. Choosing fear is the dull, dark, uninspired, and lazy way. It is not powerful. It is separated, hidden thinking.

Love is clarity. Love is giving. Love is inclusive. Love is outreach. Love is flexibility. Love is flow. It is the exact opposite of fear.

I encourage you to start choosing Love as a new approach to life. Start choosing Love consciously. See what happens to your life. Choose Love, then close your eyes. Picture your heart opening. You will be amazed at the feeling. It is a taste of Heaven. Do it a hundred times a day. You will feel a tingle from your head to your shoulders the more often you do this. This helps to release the God-energy in you, the energy that is your birthright as a Child of God.

What you focus on eventually happens. It is part of your inner power. If it doesn't happen immediately, keep with it. Eventually the Love will break through. It is present within each and every one of my Children.

All of my Children — and I do mean ALL of them are perfectly, spiritually blessed. Grace is not for just "some" of my Children. Heaven does not put up walls. Heaven takes down walls.

HAPPINESS AND DEPRESSION

When your life gets tired, when you are not replenishing the Love energy within you, you can become depressed. A lowness of spirit can set in. All you need to do is change the energy cycle. Stop momentarily doing things for yourself. See to someone else's comfort, someone else's happiness. Find a way to give service. The energy will change very quickly. Try it and see if this is not true.

Do not look toward drugs to solve your depression. Drugs will only mask the depression symptoms.

We all come from The Father – like sparks of the Divine. He is the Light and the Fuel of Love itself. When you realize the preciousness of your connection to Him, you will rejoice every hour of each day. You will realize how

SAFE you are in your destiny. You can then dissolve all the old fears. Notice I do not say "put your fears away." That implies you might bring them out again when the world's fear consciousness magnetizes you again. "Dissolve" means they disappear into the nothingness from where they came.

EASE AND STRUGGLE

You would be amazed at how many wonderful, talented, beautiful Souls only know how to keep repeating the past. They keep duplicating their own past out of fear. They do this out of timidness, out of boredom, out of fear of change. They do not know how to change the pattern and are afraid to open their lives to Christ and His Light. It is the story of many earthly lives.

Struggle can be a habit. How refreshing it is when young children and teens decide not to follow the energy patterns of their struggling parents. They create their lives anew. And what happens? Perhaps they experience Lightness. Prosperity. Fun. Look to the new generation for freshness, excitement, and new possibilities. When youths have no idea what *won't* work for them, they create a new life out of freshness and originality. Life thrives on open-mindedness and new ideas! I encourage all my Children to be fresh and creative this way.

Whether you are at the start of adult life, half way through, or reaching life's culmination, you deserve the newness of Love every day. When you choose Love, you give from an open heart.

Try to meet new people with a different energy, with a different vitality. Some people feed on the excitement of life and its opportunities, thus they open up new life for themselves. They can be very helpful to you.

Many individuals have built their Heaven on earth out of a spirit of vitality. They create a new life for themselves out of Love. There is a certain drive – a vision – a hope. With this energy, people can rise above the system's limitations.

Try not to live with the idea of injustice. It will only saddle you with a mental prison about "the injustice of the system." If you live with hope, you will have hope. If you live with Love in your hearts, then you will be Love. We are all creators. Our Father made you so that you can create your own life.

PRAYING ON THE JOURNEY

Many people get lost on the journey. Some of them come to me. Some of them are ritualistic – they Light candles in my honor. They pray. They cry in the darkness. And if there is a prayer in their heart, a belief in something bigger than themselves that is all Love, then that Love can come to them. Love transforms.

The point is that they are reaching out beyond themselves for something greater. And I am there for them. Others who do not know how to pray – or who believe that prayer does not work – can learn how to extend themselves in different ways. All prayers are answered. Prayers are for the benefit of those who pray. Prayer is a creative act. There are many creative ways to pray. Using creativity in this area can free you up tremendously.

Then, there are those who are temporarily stuck. And there are also those who are stuck "long term." Either can be helped. A simple little miracle, a new point of view, can change it all. And it can all change quickly. All it takes is a little willingness, a little Grace.

But you must ask for help. A prayer. A thought. Pray to me, to Christ, to the Holy Spirit, to your angels. Ask for help. We cannot ignore a genuine request for help.

Prayer with hope and Love will help to loosen your Soul. It will help your Soul to fly. I am here in the presence of this book to help you. Let my words here serve as a healing balm for tired Souls who are afraid to try again. Souls afraid that they might lose. Afraid they might make "fools" of themselves. Afraid of life itself, waiting for it to be over, so they can let go of the pain and frustration in death. This is no answer.

Whatever is not dealt with in life must be handled after death. There is no escaping the journey of the Soul. The Soul is evolving toward Love. Your earth experience is the place to learn this lesson. The time is NOW. Now is all there is.

You can only realize your Grace and Love in the present. The future is an illusion. There is only a long string of "nows." This is your life. I would suggest that you take possession of it. Try Love in the NOW. It works.

DEATH AND THE AFTERLIFE

The death you ask about…the death you fear…allow me to tell you in all simplicity: There is no death, my Children. So you can rest your fears. There is simply a change in levels. Of course, to some of my Children, change is as frightening as death. To those Children I say: You need change to alleviate fear and to help you stretch toward Joy.

Remember, the Soul never dies. As a creation of God, you simply change form. You are here on earth for a very important mission – to choose Love. You should pay attention to my words here. This is your mission. I will go into more detail as to how to achieve Love, because the reward in choosing Love is to achieve Heaven on earth.

Sickness is not a prerequisite for passing into death. You can pass into death as easily and beautifully as a white cloud drifting across a blue sky. In your sleep…While sitting quietly in a chair…gently…And when you pass on, your loved ones should celebrate your passing quietly, gently, with reverence…remembering your Soul with respect. You do not cry for the passing of a rose from a tight bud to a full blossom, with gently falling petals. Likewise, death is no reason to cry. Death is a time to accept the change – with Peace in your heart.

After death, you do not "fall" to a lower level of non-existence, into darkness or lost-ness. Rather, you are greeted…welcomed…to your new level. It is more like walking across a green, open pasture until you reach a river with your teachers and friends. It is very beautiful and tranquil.

But I must tell you – you take with you whatever level you achieved with the Holy Spirit during life. If you led a life rich with wonderful experiences of

Joy, they become part of you. If you chose Love, you will take that Love with you.

On the other hand, if you were dull in life, if you were lazy and took from life, you will bring that with you into the next level. You will not cross the green pasture with the same Joy in your heart. You are here to experience, to give, to Love – and with these decisions made for Love, you leave with Love.

SUICIDE

Suicide is one of the saddest of human endings for a great number of reasons. Primarily, suicide is almost always a story of separation. It is often the story of a Soul who lost faith. Faith in God, faith in oneself, faith in friends, faith in the world, faith in one's Higher Self. The separation I speak of is sad because of the isolation and loneliness that often precedes suicide.

Why is it that in a world teaming with people, with help, with ways to love and to serve…that a Soul could come to a dead end? Why is a dead end the ultimate stopping place? Does one not have free choice to turn around and choose another road? Is there not always the capacity to choose again?

Some people choose not to choose. And that is a decision in itself.

Others choose to turn their back on the world – to reject the world. That is a statement in itself. Oftentimes, suicide is played out because of a deep hurt. People who commit suicide are often very sensitive Souls. Because of their conditioning they often see a world that rejects them, a world that is cruel, insensitive, and mean. Their reaction is to turn their backs on the world they feel has hurt or deserted them.

But in the twinkling of an eye they could have changed their mind and chosen not to go there. They could have chosen Love.

What happens to a Soul that commits suicide? Often the answer is remedial work. Just like a Child who has to repeat a grade, the person who commits suicide still has to learn particular lessons of Love.

People sometimes take their own life because they can no longer bear the pain. And from that point on they may choose to learn their lessons through

Love instead of pain. It is their privilege to reprogram their learning pattern from pain to Love. Ultimately, these Souls still must learn the real lesson – to make all their decisions based on Love. That is the reason why each and every Soul is on earth. Please remember, this is an art and a discipline of the heart.

It is important to realize that people who choose suicide are not punished by God. Yet, in another way, these Souls are punishing themselves. Living a life on earth is a privilege. It is a chance to learn many lessons quickly – lessons about choosing Love. Each Soul was brought into the world, raised, educated and given the opportunity to Love. Suicide is turning one's back on Love. But it is a choice.

Another point of view is this: Each Soul has Free Will, and each Soul always does the perfect thing for its advancement. So you could always say that for them suicide was the perfect expression for that Soul at that time of its existence. That way their action is not judged by us. And they are blessed for being the perfect Souls that they undoubtedly are.

Older individuals who choose to take their own life to spare themselves the pain or embarrassment of aging or of terminal illness should always have a discussion first with the Holy Spirit, their Inner Teacher. If their lesson is one in which this is the most loving thing to do, then we must respect their Free Will, since each Soul is a perfect creation of God. Each Soul is always in charge of its own destiny. Even the law of the world cannot dictate in this area. Sometimes there is a nobility to this type of Free Will. Sometimes, not. But in any event – who are we to judge? We never can know the path of another Soul. Let us not judge those who commit suicide. Let us always send them Love to wherever they are on their journey.

STAYING SAFE IN TODAY'S WORLD

The media makes us constantly aware of evil in the world – the destruction, the hopelessness of the human situation. It is up to you to choose how you want to react. I urge you to choose Love. From where I am on this plane, it is hard for me to see evil. Seeing evil is a judgment. Seeing evil requires fear.

If I choose no evil, then evil need not exist for me.

You are only vulnerable if you want to be vulnerable. If you insist on being fearful out of habit, you could possibly attract to you exactly what it is that you fear. If you wish to be safe in Heaven while you're on earth, you can be safe in Heaven while on earth. The latter is a decision of Love. You have simply forgotten that you are a perfect Child of God with great creativity. Random violence seldom visits anyone in my mantle of Grace.

You are free to choose to be safe. If you choose the path of Love and safety, and you do not place yourself in positions of extreme vulnerability, you can pass through life on earth relatively unscathed. You have that freedom of will as a benefit of being a Child of God.

If you live in a city or environment where you feel you are in danger, then your own consciousness can protect you, gently. You can go out in the day, interact with Love – be lighthearted and enjoy life. But exercise discernment for your general safety. Perhaps it is wiser not to wander about the city at night alone. You would be safe if you are protected by Grace. But if you are truly loving to yourself you will respect certain laws of safety.

Dangers can be mis-created by your own point of view. They can be destructive to your own sense of well-being. They will eventually need to be dissolved as part of your Undoing.

JESUS AND THE RIGHT EMPHASIS

Regarding my Son, Jesus, some feel that His crucifixion was one of the major factors in His life, and that it overshadowed everything else. To believe that is to focus on guilt and fear. My Son, Jesus Christ, lived a wonderful life. He was a great teacher. He was admired and adored by His followers. His message and teachings were beautifully accomplished. His end was a part of His teaching ministry.

Perhaps it is true that on the last day of His life Jesus was under physical pain and duress. But He did not live His life in agony. On a spiritual level, there is always the choice of how to accept an experience. Jesus accepted the circumstance of pain and responded, "Father, forgive them. They know not what they do." He chose to live his crucifixion from a spirit of Love. Thus, the pain did not victimize Jesus. He was above that, for He was a Soul at Peace and in Peace.

Jesus died not as a victim, but as part of a process. The important part of His process was His Resurrection, His new life! It was an important part of demonstrating His continuity of life. That was long ago. If He re-lived the story today for the benefit of teaching, the process might be very different. Man is at a different stage of development today. The teaching experience decided on with the Holy Spirit is ALWAYS appropriate to the situation.

FREE WILL FOR HEAVEN

Your Father created each of you as perfect and innocent Children of God. But most important, He created each of you with your own Free Will. Each person has to make their his or her own decision to return to Him, to the Father in Heaven, out of Love. My Son, Jesus Christ, chose to return to Heaven. So must it be with you. Heaven is a decision you must make for yourself. You must consciously decide you wish to return home to your Father. That is because of your gift of Free Will. Because of your Free Will, each one of you, as a Child of God, must consciously DECIDE that you want to return to Heaven. That conscious decision is a choice that I am urging you to make. You make it by choosing Love in every continuing moment of your life.

The word "sin" means missing the mark, making the wrong choice, time and again. Listen to your Inner Partner and Teacher, the Holy Spirit. Examine your heart as to why you do things. Intent is everything. If you find you are stuck in life, then perhaps your life decisions are not based on Love. Perhaps you are doing the right things for the wrong reasons. Or perhaps you are doing the wrong things for the right reasons. If that is so, then change your decisions. You have to make the choice of doing the right things for the right reasons. The Holy Spirit, Jesus Christ and I can help you to do this. All you need do is ask.

Part Six

On Sex & Sexuality

SEX AND SEXUALITY ARE AN IMPORTANT PART OF YOUR LIFE AS a human being. It should not be denied as if it did not exist. Sex is nothing to cause embarrassment. God created you, and sexuality is one of His pleasant gifts for human beings. Please realize, my Children, that sex and sexuality, if handled with the right attitude, can be beautiful, creative, and pleasurable. There is nothing wrong with enjoying pleasure for its own sake. It is part of the nurturing process, nurturing Self and nurturing others in an intimate way.

If people would just relax a little more in life, instead of trying to keep so busy, they would have more Peace in their lives. You each need Peace in your lives, as well as pleasure. Heaven itself is a very pleasurable and beautiful non-physical state. It is a Joy to be here. But it can be a Joy to be on earth, too.

Enhance your life whenever possible. Take time for yourself. Do not let your life become tired, mundane or stale. Give yourself the permission to live life in a variety of new and exciting ways. If my Children could learn to comfort themselves with sex while on earth, and if they could do so without guilt – it would make it easier for them to achieve the Kingdom of Heaven. Sex should be fun, but still sacred. It should bring deep Peace. It is possible to combine these two aspects.

I am speaking about sex with discernment. Do nothing to violate the sacredness of sex. Sex within a marriage is fine. Sex alone is acceptable. But I am not advocating any form of random sex with other people's partners. Do not confuse relationships. If people could realize the sacredness, the creativeness and beauty of sex – it would help their state of mind.

Sex is a heightened awareness. It can be holy and fun and have great purity at the same time. That is why I am advocating that it be encouraged on earth.

Sex with Love elevates the Spirit, whether with a partner or alone. There is such a range of beautiful emotions that a Soul can have while experiencing sex. It requires discipline and higher energies to bring new creative thoughts to lovemaking. You have the power to choose to experience your lovemaking with Joy, sensitivity, and great Peace.

Love is the very energy of God. You allow Love to pass through your life. So it is with sex: You can allow the beautiful, quiet spirituality of Love to flow to you through sex.

Chastity is extremely important for young people. They should not experiment with partnered sex until they are mature enough to develop a deeper relationship. Partnered sex should not start out young. If teens start out with sex for sex's sake with pure physicality and no depth of emotion, they may never grasp the sacredness or the depth of sex. It may always be just beyond them, and they will keep wondering: "Is that all?"

Sex should be used for Love, for well-being, for Joy, for health, and for enhancement of life. Sex should embody both beauty and Peace. View yourself as the sacred entity that you are – as a Child of God. Realize that sexual pleasures are desirous, and that they can also be Soul-enhancing.

The pleasures you enjoy in sex are not wasted. Nothing of Joy or beauty that goes into the universe is ever wasted – a baby's laugh…the scent of a beautiful flower…or the enjoyment of pleasure in sex. It adds to the amount of Love in the universe. So the expression *"Make Love, not War,"* is definitely something that you should think about.

There should not be guilt about having sex alone. This is acceptable. People often need this for a release and a balance in their lives. Even this can have a Peace and a holiness. Again, it should be done with love and dignity. God created you as a reflection of His own Being. He created everything about you as part of His creative energy. In all that I say to you: Remember, you are never truly alone. Your angels and your highest guiding Self are always close by. Always do everything in your life with great Love and they will be pleased.

It is unnatural to expect to have no sex or pleasure. This keeps the human system very highly strung. It can cause frustration and unusual behavior. We are no longer caught in the sacrifice paradigm of the martyr. That paradigm existed for many centuries, but today we are in the era of a spirituality that is creative. It is not what you *don't* do that counts. It is what you DO with your time and your life that counts.

ABUSE

Abusing Children through sexual acts is one of the most heinous and terrible acts occurring on earth. It scars Children mentally – boys and girls – and requires a tremendous amount of healing from the Holy Spirit. Each Child is a perfect, innocent Child of God, as you are a perfect and innocent Child of God. Never, never, NEVER harm another young Soul through a sexual act with one of my Children. Never persuade young, vulnerable Souls to do anything that is out of character for their age, sex or innocence.

Never hurt another Soul because of your sexual needs and maneuvering. Never have twisted ideas of expressing sexual love to a Child. Leave Children alone with regard to sex. I cannot state more clearly or with more conviction.

It is so important to the life of young Children to be brought up safely! Those who engage Children for their own selfish pleasures are hurting *themselves* far, far beyond their comprehension.

PORNOGRAPHY

Pornography is an old, archaic behavior pattern. It is sad that it is still so alive today. This is a case of lower vibration mentality based on demeaning others for a false sense of superiority. It is a primitive form of amusement, demeaning to our Higher Selves.

As people mature and develop in their civilization, these older forms of base entertainment will dissolve. Until then, it is beneficial to spare young minds from low life behavior patterns. I urge you to spare the exposure of your sons and daughters from any form of pornography, because it is responsible for rape, abhorrent thinking and all types of animalistic behavior that has no place in an evolving civilization.

While some people may enjoy pornography for its raciness or rawness, the other side of the situation is that it panders to the lower side of youths whom we are trying to raise up in consciousness. With many of the "Indigo Children" being born into the world as spiritual leaders, you will hopefully find less interest in pornography in the future. As my Children evolve, pornography will sink back into the low levels from which it came. We will all be the happier for it. Until that time, know where to draw the line in protecting consciousness.

SHARING LOVE THROUGHOUT THE COSMOS

Every wonderful feeling is enjoyed as an energy form throughout the universe, cumulatively speaking. As an example, Joy is not wasted. When you experience Joy or happiness, it does not just dissolve. The Joy is recycled throughout the cosmos, so to speak. So is happiness, mirth, pleasure, playfulness, and Love. When you reach a certain point on your spiritual path, you will not have to contend with fear. All of life can be an extreme pleasure. I cannot tell you what a wonderful, free feeling this will be for you.

A perfect day, here or on earth, should be spent in Love, gratitude, laughter, outreach, pleasure, happiness and Joy. You will spend time teaching and reaching out to others. And you will also take the time to be loving to yourself. See if you can reach the point where the only emotions you experience are Love, gratitude, laughter, outreach, pleasure, happiness and Joy. Then you will experience Heaven on earth. In this way you will always be contributing to the universe.

LIFE MOVES FAST IN TODAY'S WORLD

You have the choice of how fast your life will move. You need not be pushed by the fear consensus of the world. You need not pick up the stress you feel in today's world. Rushing is not an excuse for living. You are a Child of God with great spirituality and magnificence to your being. Do not live your life as if you were part of a *race*. Take the time for your inner Peace. You are the one who makes the decision to slow down and live your life with an inner reverence and Peace.

To create your own Peace, simplify your life. Choose the principles that resonate with your beliefs. They may be principles you have within that you have never truly explored. They may take some self-examination to bring them to the surface. But if your current set of principles has brought you to where you are…shouldn't you consider making some changes?

HOMOSEXUALITY

Homosexuality is a topic that cannot be ignored in today's world. But it would be so much better if fear did not surround this topic. While throughout history there has been constant judgment of homosexuality, it has evolved considerably in the last fifty years. Those who have a broad awareness of homosexuality today understand that it is simply a preference. It is so much easier if we are not judgmental on an issue like this. We can allow people their space without having an opinion.

A new wave of acceptance of homosexuality has been occurring around the world in recent years. This represents progress for our world, because each time an old fear dissolves, the stronger we become. Allowing the idea of homosexuality, or a bi-sexual nature, without having to participate in it, or to have an opinion about it, is a step forward toward freedom.

Sexual preferences are but temporary illusions that people go through on their journey through life. It is not necessary for us to judge, nor to give forth an opinion on such topics. Some people may react to homosexuality with horror, squeamishness or fear. But there is no need for fear in this regard. Such fear, or homophobia, may be left over from the past when individuals could be severely chastised or killed for homosexual behavior. Fortunately, today's world has evolved far beyond this type of fearful punishing.

Whenever there is fear, or bitterness or hate, there is lack of Love. So neither Love nor Christ can be there. Choose not to judge others. It is not necessary for you to have an opinion on everything. Try *not* to have an opinion on everything. If you do not live in judgment, then the Holy Spirit's gentle Voice can be heard. It is the only way that spiritual growth can occur.

As gay roles evolve, people will come to understand that their lifestyles are simply another way of playing out life situations, another framework for learning life's lessons. And gays will hopefully continue to evolve as contributors to our society, taking on a more visible and responsible role in the future.

Remember, too, that both gay and heterosexual roles are important to your society and to yourselves as a way of developing. Do not ignore their value to you. You can choose to be very creative within these parameters. As humans you may be tempted to stray from the norm because of your fascination with something that is different. Try not to choose a gay role simply because of its novelty to you. Respect the value of the norm. If you were born a homosexual, you cannot do much to change your orientation. You must live it out. If you were born with a heterosexual orientation, then you must live that out, authentically. If you were born with a bi-sexual orientation, you have a path that may be even more difficult to live out. It is important for you to live out your role in this world that is part of your individual lifepath. In following this, you will come up with the proper lessons. If you are gay and you choose to hide it and live a heterosexual life, life's lessons may not be as on target for you and you may often feel disoriented. Many people do this because they fear the stigma of being different. It takes courage to be authentic on earth. People who ridicule others for being authentic are short on understanding. They, too, in time will grow as they learn their lessons of Love. In the meantime, it is good discipline for all of us not to pass judgment on gay relationships.

RELATIONSHIPS

Relationships are one of life's greatest comforts. No matter what stage of development you are in with the Holy Spirit, you can attract to yourself the perfect partner for learning and loving for that particular time. If you enter into the relationship with discernment, but without fear, you can nurture Love. When you feel safe with a new partner, try opening your heart, and see if they respond by opening theirs. If they are capable of opening their heart, you can have a wonderful relationship.

On the other hand, if your new partner in a relationship is not capable of opening their heart to you, you will still be lonely, even in this relationship. So you might ask yourself the important question: Why begin a relationship if the relationship will still leave me empty? Do I just need someone's physical presence? The opening up of one's heart to Love is the whole point of living. Keep looking for that element in your relationships.

It is also important to remember that it is not within your power to change an individual. Only the Holy Spirit working from within can effect a true change by working intimately with a Soul. The Soul must always have the freedom to make choices of its own Free Will. I will focus on relationships in a later book that will concern Love and relationships.

PEOPLE WHO UPSET YOU

There may be some people who give you problems and whom you dread seeing. They may upset you deeply. Perhaps they attack you. Always watch these situations consciously. Be awake. See what it is in them that causes fear in you. Often these people – difficult as they may be – are like red flags because they can point out areas of yourself that need healing.

Do not run away from these people who infuriate you. Do not fight with them because they can provide important answers for you. These people can be your BEST teachers. Thank them inwardly. They will show you the unhealed parts of your Soul so that you can heal yourself in conjunction with your Inner Teacher, the Holy Spirit. There is something within yourself that you see – that you cannot stand to see – that you are trying to keep hidden. These persons may draw out the worst in you and show you the dark side of yourself that you try to keep hidden; and *that is precisely why they are valuable*.

Once you are healed, once you are balanced in Love, you will perceive them quite differently. You may see their shortcomings quite differently. You will be able to experience Peace in their presence, and they will probably react differently to you. As you give Love, you will find Love reflected back from them.

Sometimes, even after you have healed, these people will still upset you, just because of the way they are. In those cases, it is acceptable for you to move on and to choose not to be in their presence. This can always be done with Love. You will know you have grown past them and learned your lessons of Love when you can make the decision to leave their presence without it upsetting you.

LASTING MARRIAGES

Older generations from another era were more content with life – more satisfied with life the way it was. They were often fulfilled with less. Many people of earlier eras had a more formal discipline to their lives. They did not have all the options that people have in today's world. Today's generation has become much more mobile – and more privileged, in a way. This is true throughout the world. Communications and the way people work have changed the world tremendously. Many people used to stay married out of dependency for each other.

But today's viewpoint often seems to be: "If it's not working, let's end the relationship and begin anew."

A pattern of mental discernment needs to be developed here. Some important questions need to be asked about a poor relationship:

Is it because of me?

Is it because of my partner?

Is it because of someone outside the marriage?

Is it because of something in the outside world?

A large proportion of the time an important part of the equation is the first question: Is it because of me?

If the problem lies within you, even if you replace a partner, the problem will probably repeat itself. Because *wherever you go, there you are*. You cannot run away from yourself. If your thinking is in error, then the problem is portable. That is why some Souls have a long string of marriages, and their same old mistakes keep repeating. Work on question number one. It is easier to solve a problem at its source.

In earlier generations, divorce was not as available an option. People were taught to learn from their strife. They often lived with a sense of resignation and silent sacrifice. Divorce, until more recently, was not an option except for the very rich. And, often, people stayed together for the sake of the family. There was often more self-sacrifice than there is today.

Today's younger people live life with many more options. However, they have just as many problems today due to separated ideas. They often have more problems, even though their range of choices is wider. With all these options, the world is becoming more and more complex. Children often live in more than one home, with additional stepmothers and stepfathers. They often live in blended families. The forms expand. But there is often much Love and harmony in these new family relationships.

All the recent divorces of the past few decades are causing much more respect for good marriages among young people. The next generation will see much more stability in family life. The divorce generation has caused these Children to respect Peace, togetherness, and harmony in relationships.

These broken relationships have caused a residue of considerable sadness in the world. When so many marriage relationships fail, that cumulatively adds up to a great deal of sadness, grief, and mourning for the Love that was lost – or might have been. Who heals all this sadness? Where does it go? Like smoke in a closed room, it leaves a residue.

Your world is suffering more from sadness, depression, and loneliness than it is from physical imbalances. In addition to having consciousness about recycling in the physical environment, have consciousness about recycling Love throughout the world.

And often – even after a divorce – the heart of the problem still exists within. So the healing still must take place – within your heart. The Holy Spirit has been helping to heal the brokenness and separation of all these divorced, hurt, and often disappointed adults. But within all this, there have been many valuable learning experiences and considerable growth that takes place as part of the process.

You can never force a mate to heal against his or her will. If a marriage environment becomes hostile to your well-being, often you cannot continue to live in an atmosphere of bitterness – without love. So divorce becomes necessary for both parties – and for the Children, if there are Children in the marriage. Divorce sometimes becomes necessary out of the need for mental Peace and safety.

Of course it is always possible to heal hurt, to heal the neglect, to heal the misunderstandings. Miracles happen every day. People do change from within. Love will always offer you good reasons and ways to stay in Grace.

Try to realize that it takes some people a long, long time to change. They are deeply trapped within their lower selves. You cannot control their will if they are adamant about staying stuck. And remember that each case should be approached on an individual basis. Do not call your relationship Love if the Love has dissolved. There are times in life to let go, to forgive and to move on. There are always new fields of Love.

Seldom has man known such a civilized world of human rights as today. The individual has rights and is often treated with dignity. Be grateful. It was not always this way.

Learn to see marriage as a gift that two people give to each other. Each Child of God is perfect and complete. A Soul does not NEED to enter into marriage. There are other ways to absorb your loneliness and provide for growth. People should enter into marriage as a gift to each other – a gift of all that they are.

A good marriage is two people coming together to form a new entity – two complete Souls. And, with a marriage, the totality is always greater than the sum of its parts. Two people together offer each other the gift of mutual Grace. Mutual growth. Two people giving. Two people loving. Two Souls in union, in harmony and in Peace. This can be bliss when it is in balance.

But marriage is not about giving up yourself to the relationship, of becoming less of an individual. Try not to lose yourself in a relationship. Rather, FIND yourself within the stability of a relationship. You have the responsibility to be the unique, many-faceted reflection of God that you are. Search for your individual gifts and share them. That is an important part of your quest in life.

ABOUT DIVORCE

Divorce has been a painful area for so many of my Children. It is a very important area for us to consider.

Each Soul is a perfect Child of God. Regardless of what you might consider to be "sins" or errors in your life, God made you perfect, and you are still perfect and innocent, even if you cannot understand or believe the truth at the level where you are.

It is the obligation and privilege of each Child of God to see himself or herself as a complete Soul, a totally perfect Child of God.

If two Souls can come together, complete in themselves, and enhance the existence of one another through a union called matrimony, this can be a strong growth relationship for both parties. They can support each other in growth and in Love. Such marriages are based in Heaven. Some marriages start out that way. Other marriages grow into that kind of a loving relationship. In either situation, it can be a great blessing.

But the difficulty is that many people enter into marriage and then proceed to give much of themselves away. This is not what you are asked to do, to become less than what you are. In the long run this will only breed resentment, limitation and unhappiness. Again I say, you are meant to be the complete Soul that you are. Marriage is not intended to be an exercise in self-sacrifice. That was the Old Testament way, not the New Testament way that is grounded in Love.

Where marriages are concerned, many people do not pray enough or listen enough. For a good marriage you should select a mate who will be an enhancement to your Soul and your personal development.

If you have a deep listening relationship with the Holy Spirit and live in an aura of Truth, it is easier to find the right type of mate for you. You need someone whose spiritual pathway intersects with yours. You cannot always see how that will play out. I might stress that it often takes patience. Great matches do not always happen overnight. Remember, I was once a Jewish mother, and thus matchmaking is still of interest to me. I can be of help to you in this regard. Simply ask me, soulfully, in your prayers.

In some relationships, people can be very mismatched, and feel even more lonely within the relationship than they would if alone. When there is such an imbalance…when the marriage is no longer a loving environment in which to live…when meanness or violence enters… it becomes difficult for continued growth to occur. Peace and harmony occur less and less frequently. In such instances, remember that your first obligation is to be kind and loving to yourself. Be gentle to the Divinity within you. The Holy Spirit is always with you as your Teacher. Listen to Him.

He will probably remind you that you can learn either by pain and suffering, or by Love. How you choose to approach the situation is your choice. If the situation is unworkable, choose Love. Be kind to yourself. Let go.

This does not mean to be nasty. It does not mean to be aggressive and attacking to the other Soul. It means to choose Love. To let go. To move on with life.

On the other hand, if you are the kind of person who likes to learn through suffering and sacrifice, you are free to continue on in that way. While it is not your obligation, or your business, to change another Soul (remember, that is the Holy Spirit's province, to work from within), you may still try to influence that Soul by an example of Love. But you are not bound to do so.

There is no need to feel great life-long guilt about a marriage that did not work. Part of the forgiveness process is of letting go of the past. One should move on to a loving, nurturing environment that works for the Souls involved. Perhaps the choice is to be single. Perhaps it is to be married. That is between you and the Holy Spirit and your life lesson. Love yourself and be careful not to repeat the same mistake.

WHAT GOD HAS PUT TOGETHER

My Children, please remember that God does not act as a Divine matchmaker. People match themselves through their own Free Will. They take their own personal responsibility for entering into a marriage with another Soul, and they may take the same initiative in leaving a marriage.

Consider the phrase "What God has put together, let no man put asunder."

Consider that this phrase may refer more to the Children in a marriage. God, Christ, and the Holy Spirit are often quite instrumental in effecting the parent and Child union in a loving marriage. Children do not receive their parents accidentally. This is a Divinely appointed process that matches a Child with the parents that are best suited to nurture that Soul.

Each one of the parents is responsible for the Child that they helped to bring into the world. They are both an important part of the maturing and development process of that Child, all the way through life. They owe it to that Child to be available, not just physically, but to open their hearts whenever that Child is in need.

"What God has put together, let no man put asunder" may refer more to the ongoing parental-child responsibility. The support of each Child, mentally, physically, and emotionally is a lifelong obligation of both parents, whether they are married or divorced or remarried. Even if a parent is estranged from a Child for any reason, there are still ways of reaching out – calls, loving letters, prayers. The responsibility for begetting a Child is lifelong.

The words I would stress here are loyalty and non-judgment. Loyalty to the Child and to the Self. Non-judgment of the Child and of the Self. The capital letters signify the Child within that is the Child of God. And the Self within that is the Higher Self.

And so, if this phrase refers more to the parent-child union established by God, then it may not refer as much to marriage and divorce. Consider this from a loving viewpoint. It may help to dispel some of the guilt that surrounds divorce. In many divorces, people had to do what they had to do. It was the only way they could be loving to themselves. The answer is always based on Love. So please, do *not* feel guilt over divorce. Stable, loving marriages are the ideal. But often, adjustments are necessary for the growth of all Souls involved.

Part Seven

Money & Support in Life

MY FRIENDS, THE STORY OF MONEY IS THE STORY OF LIFE. HOW YOU live life – the creativity of decisions, of Love, of giving, of your personal generosity. These things have everything to do with the way money flows to you. Your flow of money also has much to do with your most basic thoughts about money and support. You formed your thoughts about money when you were a child, and if you picked up any fearful ideas, that fear can keep money from circulating freely in your life.

My Children usually choose to learn their lessons in life through one of three ways: with relationships, health problems, or money issues. When all three occur simultaneously, this condition can bring suffering into your life. If this happens to you the question should always be: What is my lesson here? How can I choose Love to solve these problems? *The answer is always Love,* no matter where you are stuck.

You may feel victimized by the human system. Perhaps you have pressing debts. Perhaps you can never find enough work at a high enough level of pay. Perhaps your job has been eliminated. These problems may take a while to solve, but they can be solved, and solved through Love. Trust in me. Ask for my help. I will bring you comfort and the presence of Love in which all problems are solved.

Try to never see yourself as being a victim of money. In truth, you can create money all the time if your frame of mind is correct. Depending on how you think, you might be creating abundance, or you might be creating scarcity. In either case, you are creating.

If you do not like what is happening in your life with regard to money, step back, observe what is happening, and try to create a loving change within yourself. This may be harder than it sounds for some of you. It sometimes takes much discipline to change the "money maps" that you have in your mind. Ask the Holy Spirit for guidance.

Some of my Children are very gentle and are not assertive enough about money in the world. They do not understand how the world works. They may be afraid to ask for what they want. Or they do not know what they want. In any case, the situation can be changed. No one has to be stuck in one position.

Most people who have money are very defined. They know what they want. They have no qualms about stating their Truth about it. They do not consider money to be magic. Because, of course, it is not. Money is just a medium of exchange. Money is energy. To love money for its own sake, however, is to make it sacred, to put it on a pedestal. If you love money too much, it can cause you considerable problems. Do not love the money itself. Love the energy that the exchange of money can produce.

As you know, there are many people who are prosperous. They are happy. They have all the things that really "count" in life. But they do not have enough money to handle all their obligations. There are many people like this in today's world. The ego world pays for very specific types of services, goods, and information. It is helpful to be clever enough to understand the system and to know where to contribute and gain reward. It helps if you can find your gift – what you are good at – what you love to do.

Trust your natural abilities. Find ways that you can contribute – ways the world will support. *You are the writer of your own story in life.* If you do not like the way your story is written, re-write it. Choose differently. But always choose with Love!

Please, my Children, take comfort in one important Truth. No one is destined to be poor while another is destined to be rich. Perhaps you chose to be poor to learn some lessons while on earth. But if you do not like where you are, you are free to make the decision to change. Nothing is forever on earth. Life is a constancy of change. You are never stuck. Your Free Will gives you fluidity of decision. You can always change your mind.

EARNING A LIVELIHOOD

I would like you to remember the phrase: "Give a man a fish and he eats for a day…Teach a man to fish and he eats for a lifetime." There is much Truth in that statement that applies to your world today. So many people of talent are looking for a way of doing meaningful work whereby they can earn a living: young people who do not know what to do with their lives…older people who have retired early or been forced out of a job. They have so much to give. Give them attention. Help them find a way to be of service, and at the same time, to make a decent living in this world. This will require creativity on your part, but it is very feasible to create new situations – new opportunities – for people with ordinary or extraordinary talents who can contribute and be paid decently for their work.

In recent decades, throughout the world, there has been an activity called "downsizing." This has forced many people out of jobs for the sake of higher profitability. The importance of the "bottom line" has a certain deceit about it. It is more about selfishness (greed) than anything else. It is not where my

Children should be going. You should be going for the "top line." That is about embracing, rather than squeezing out.

In the past, many more businesses took care of their workers, like a family. There was a sense of responsibility towards one's fellow man. What has become of this? This is one of the elements of "backsliding" that I mentioned earlier. It is one of the ways that my Children are misaligning their values. When businesses exist for the profitability of the few, this is selfishness. Selfishness is a backward choice. It is not about choosing Love. It is not inclusive. Selfishness is about exclusivity and separation.

When my Children play the selfish game in their personal life, the consequences are bad enough. But when they play the selfish game as part of a group effort, such as with a large corporation, with their government, their church or a charitable institution, the damage they do to their psyche can be considerable. They may not go to a physical hell, but they can put themselves into a mental hell that will have long-term consequences to their well-being and their Soul.

Individuals who may appear to be "winners" in the world are sometimes slipping backward in their own evolution. There is a price they pay in their own consciousness for excessive selfish behavior – especially when they are at the helm of responsibility.

Just because "everyone does it," just because "that's the way business is done" is not an excuse to continue. There is a personal liability that comes from being in a position of responsibility over other people. Misusing that position brings a complex set of consequences. Forgiveness is possible, of course. But each Soul has a responsibility to contribute to the Undoing. Those who keep creating selfishness are moving against the grain. They diminish their Soul content.

There is so much emphasis on money in your culture. Money has become a god to many people. What money can buy. How money can insulate. How money can provide security. Please wake up!

Unless the emphasis of your life is on giving and outreach, you are going in the wrong direction.

Money can be used for outreach, for sharing, for expansion, for inclusion. That is the direction in which businesses and people should be moving. That is evolutionary thinking.

SPECIALNESS AS A BE-ALL IN YOUR CULTURE

Many of the world's cultures have lost ground during the last few decades because of the monetary culture. This has happened because of a very old idea called "SPECIALNESS." I would like to expose the old idea of specialness for what it is.

Specialness is what occurs when one person tries to HAVE more than another. To BE more than another. To make oneself STAND OUT in some way for being MORE SPECIAL than another. This is a very old game. But many of my Children still play it. So much time and effort is wasted on these little vanities and on these BIG vanities.

Please wake up, my Children. The vain game of specialness, of trying to show off or compete, of trying to be better than your brother, is very old, and very tired, and very stupid. I say stupid because many of my Children are wasting precious time playing out their lives in this specialness-vanity game.

So many of the world's values are built on specialness. Your clothes. Your cars. Your cosmetics. Your homes. Your food. Your toys. There is nothing wrong about living a beautiful life, as long as the emphasis is not on specialness.

Some of you teach your children that ballplayers are heroes just because they make so much money – they must be really SPECIAL. At the same time that business leaders are downsizing a company and taking away jobs, they are paying themselves large salaries and benefits because they have made themselves so SPECIAL. This is wrong. These values are lopsided. We cannot make progress unless there is a shift in these values.

My message is this: Certain people are not special. EVERYONE IS SPECIAL. Everyone is a perfect Child of God. When you begin to understand that every human being is a Child of God, and you begin to honor this, then your life values will shift and you will have more Love flowing through your life. Welcome to happiness. Here is where you will find new Joy.

Try to expose the selfishness game wherever you can, especially in your own life. When you find yourself wasting time trying to create "specialness" for yourself, ask yourself if this is really what your life is about. Perhaps you can shift into seeing through the eyes of Love.

Specialness plays out in so many ways. See how the specialness game plays out in relationships, in marriages, in work, and in your entire monetary culture. Some people see themselves as part of a higher class, a higher economic level, a higher educational level. Life is not meant to be about snobbishness or economic superiority. These values take up an enormous amount of time in your lives that could be invested toward growth on your journey.

The deeper problem is that over a period of time specialness creates greed. With greed, no one can ever have enough. That is what happened with so many rulers and monarchs in the past. And that is what is still happening today on levels I do not wish to share with you. I do not wish to belabor the point here.

When my Children get beyond playing the specialness game, we can then begin to make some real progress. Together, we can begin to find places for all the people who have been forced out of the game. We can begin to feed and clothe our brothers and sisters who are also truly special, who do not fit as well into the system. This is about compassion, about empathy for our brothers and sisters.

We need to shift our young Children's values beyond the ideas of winning and losing and the money-based system of heroes. They need to know that EVERYONE IS SPECIAL. You need to help them shift beyond the perception that ballplayers are very special to the idea that teachers are also very special. The cashier at the grocery store is very special. And the refuse collector in your neighborhood is also very special. That will help to open up their hearts and see the world in a bigger perspective.

Money and compassion go together. Many people have been getting this message in the past few decades. And they live their lives unselfishly — by sharing. But many of our leaders in business and government do not have the idea yet. We need to help enlighten them, to help them evolve beyond where their thinking is clogged with ideas about special interests.

NEVER TRY TO CHANGE A BROTHER

When we see the error of a brother or sister's ways, remember that it is not our personal mission to try to change them. We can never change another person. They have to change themselves. For us to think we can change another is yet another idea based on specialness. It is not our responsibility to change a brother. We should see them and the way they are as being "perfect" for them. We need to allow them space for their evolution.

Rather, we lead by example. We show others the way – silently – by inner strength. Of course, with our own Children, we can help influence their thinking to see life in an enlightened way. This is one of the privileges of being a parent.

THE ECONOMICALLY AND SOCIALLY DISADVANTAGED

Do not judge your brothers and sisters on welfare. They are in true need of your energy and attention. Teach them how to make a living and how to support their families. By giving them self-respect, you will be living the message of Love that my Son showed you in His life.

Each of my Children deserves hope, dignity and self-worth through achievement. Working together you can do this. I urge you to start by giving up one evening of television each week. You will be amazed at how much energy you will have to share with others and the deep, deep sense of gratitude and satisfaction you will receive from this. Go to your churches and your service clubs. Be with family and friends. Contribute your time. I will, with my Son, Jesus Christ, make certain that you are paid many, many times over for whatever contributions you make.

GETTING STUCK IN LIFE

Being stuck in the midst of life happens to many of my Children. It is because of where they are on their spiritual journey. The spiritual roadmap is often obscure, so that many times my Children do not realize that getting stuck is a natural part of the journey. Never put yourself down when you are in a lost period. If you expect the worst, you will get the worst. When you become lost, often your little ego will chastise you and make you feel bad. Do not listen. If it tries to tell you that your life is meant to be a struggle – and if you accept it then, of course, life will be a struggle for you. But it needn't be. On the earth level there are no ultimate Truths, such as "life is a struggle." Life is not a struggle for everyone. Some people create beautiful lives. You should all be creating beautiful lives for yourself. Life is a mirror. It mirrors back exactly what you feel and think about inside. If you see yourself as stuck, you ARE stuck. If you see yourself as guilty, you ARE guilty.

On the other hand, if through spiritual and mental discipline, you see yourself as a Perfect Child of God, then you ARE a Perfect Child of God. If you see yourself in Heaven, then you ARE in Heaven. Such is the power of a son or daughter of God. But it doesn't come just by saying so. It takes disciplined thinking and a willingness to see through the eyes of Christ, or through the eyes of Love.

Part Eight

Victims, New Age & Drugs

ALWAYS REMEMBER, MY CHILDREN, THAT WHAT YOU FOCUS ON IS what will happen. If a significant number of my Children have an enormous fear of, and focus on, an earthquake, truly expecting one...then they could collectively cause an earthquake. On the other hand, if you focus on harmony and Peace, then you can collectively create harmony and Peace. That is why, when my Children meditate in unison all over the world, as you have many times in the past, it can create a shift. You call this critical mass. There is truth in this.

What you think about, and plan, you create. Never underestimate your powers as Children of God. However, even if an earthquake occurred, it would still be a learning experience and an opportunity to respond with Love.

Let me assure you that God the Father is planning no earthquakes for you. Nor is Jesus Christ. There is no Divine retribution from our plane. We live as Love, and as Love flows, it means that nothing will occur out of punishment or meanness from our loving section of the realm.

A demeaning phrase used by humans is "An Act of God" for anything approximating an earthquake, a hurricane, a mudslide, a flood or a natural disaster. Jesus Christ and I find the phrase "An Act of God" when applied to a disaster to be a very ignorant and insensitive term. It is a concept from the Old Testament, well before Christ. God the Father does not perpetrate disasters upon you. God is the source of all Love and Light. He is the very energy that keeps you alive and breathing.

Please reconsider rewording that phrase. Perhaps "An Accident of Nature" would be a much more accurate description of such an event. Do not do disservice to your God by attributing violent acts of nature as His Will toward you. Nothing could be further from the Truth. It perpetuates ignorance and misunderstanding.

It is our will that there be no unpleasant events that occur on the earth. Your Heavenly Father, Jesus Christ and I wish no earthquakes, no monsoons, no hurricanes, no airplane crashes, no illnesses, no floods upon you. These things happen as accidents of nature. We only wish you Peace and Love.

On the earth plane, where you are now having a human experience, and living under free will, unpleasant experiences sometimes happen. Try not to judge these experiences. Whatever happens, it is always an opportunity to react with Love.

As you grow into the new millennium, you will find the energies changing. You will find more Love expanding in the world. That means Love will be the choice of more and more Souls. It represents an evolvement that is a celestial progression. My new presence on earth will help to spur that along.

In the new millennium, those Souls who are not disposed toward Love will find the Love energy repulsive and will opt to pass out of human existence. The good news of the new millennium is that you are in for a time of Peace and ease. Health problems will improve. The world of health care will focus more on preventative and optimum health. Crime and violence will begin to disperse and dissipate. When we elevate the consciousness of human Souls and preserve the innocence of your Children, you will see an entirely new energy of Love and optimism dawn on earth.

BEING A VICTIM AND CHOOSING TO BE FREE

It is important for you to come to realize that you are not a victim of the world. Never choose to see yourself as a victim of life. By seeing yourself as a victim, it makes you powerless to exercise your Free Will. When my Son, Jesus Christ, came to earth, it was to teach you perfect and unconditional Love, which is about freedom. That is a lesson many of you are still learning.

In the figurative story of Adam and Eve in the Garden, Adam and Eve made themselves victims. Eve made herself a victim of the serpent's suggestions. She showed Adam the apple and invited Adam to eat it. Adam ate the apple of his own will and also played the part of the victim, blaming Eve for his choice. In this story, neither one of them took responsibility for their own choices. And their guilt came forth when they felt a need to clothe their bodies.

After having lived in innocence with God, they gave away their innocence. This is an example of playing the victim. They gave away their power in their choice to play the victim.

The story could have been different. Had they perceived themselves as innocent, they might have said, "Yes, God, we ate the apple. We chose to eat the apple. We are sorry for having disobeyed you and we ask your forgiveness. Will you forgive us?"

God, who is all Love and forgiveness, would have forgiven them if they were asking out of the genuineness of their hearts. Our Loving God the Father would have reacted with Love and forgiveness. All they had to do was ask.

Instead, Adam and Eve ran away and hid from God out of fear. The course of mankind has been allegorically set by the way that Adam and Eve chose to play the role of the victim. Many are still hiding from God out of their own guilt.

How do we escape this course of guilt and hiding? By choosing to set ourselves and others free by perceiving not only our own innocence, but the innocence of others. We begin to look at others differently. No matter what happened in the past, we let it go. It doesn't exist for us anymore. In freeing others, we also free ourselves. We begin to see through the eyes of Love, and we make it a habit in our lives.

In this we selectively choose to see the good, the Love, the beauty in others. We see their strengths instead of their weaknesses. And this, my Children, will set you free.

To achieve inner Peace, we need to perceive a world where we are innocent and everyone else is, too. We no longer make victims of ourselves, or others.

Once we take responsibility for our actions, for our shortcomings, for our sicknesses, for our failure of relationships, for our lack of money...THEN WE ARE FREE TO CHANGE.

But many of my Children are still in hiding, feeling guilty for *something "bad" which they never really did*. Come out into the Light. Ask forgiveness. Start fresh.

You can begin to change your old victim role by listening to me, listening to the Truth I bring to you.

As I said before, I am your good news Mother. I have come to tell you that you have a rosy future. You have nothing to fear. But you MUST decide not to play the victim role. You must see the difference here. You must take responsibility for whatever you have created in life. Then your life belongs to you. And you are free to choose whatever you wish. Make it wonderful. Your Heavenly Father and I want to see you live a wonderful life. We wish the same for your Children.

Take responsibility for your Soul and your own spiritual path. In your decision lies great power for yourself. It is time to wake up from the old dream and wear the mantle of Love and responsibility that Christ gave you. *It is a Joy to wear. It is life itself.*

Perhaps on your first few decisions, change may be a little difficult. It is always uncomfortable to change – to take a chance – to choose Love. But Love is what you are.

You ARE Love, and once you begin to make decisions in the name of Love, your life will get easier and easier. But if you decide to stay stuck, then remember – that, too, is your choice.

Think of the world as a merry-go-round. At first the merry-go-round is fun. The horses go up and down. There is music. There is nothing to do but sit and enjoy the ride.

The day-to-day hypnosis of the world is like a merry-go-round. It is fun for the first few decades...ten, twenty, thirty, forty years. But eventually the sameness of life becomes more and more tiresome. And then you must choose to respond to life's challenges, get off the merry-go-round, and do something real with your life. Contribute something to the world, however small and quiet, however great. Otherwise you will die a slow death of boredom. Life will have no point.

I feel sadness when I see so many of my talented and beautiful Children slowly dying because they are sleepwalking through life. They become victims of the repetitive process of living. Eating. Sleeping. Working. Bathing. Again and again. When my Children are caught in this repetition it becomes very hard for them to pray deeply, fervently, with an open heart. They become drugged by the sameness of life.

To get off the merry-go-round does not mean to choose a dim life of suffering and sobriety. It means to choose a real life, a colorful life of fun and passion – a fresh life that you invent and create. A life where you can play again. A life where you can truly live Love. That is what I am here to teach.

NEW AGE AND THE DEVIL

Remember, hell is not a place. It is a state of mind. Any person can lead himself to hell through a series of selfish thoughts, through separation, judgment and lack of forgiveness. And FEAR.

And remember, there is no "devil" in the old sense of that word. God the Father created you whole, along with the Free Will to decide how you will live your life.

Some of my Children are afraid of what they call their "dark side." What is the dark side, except that which has not yet been exposed to the Light? It would do you well to realize there is nothing so dark about you that you cannot hold it up to the Light. Once you do, and it is exposed as the simple darkness that it is, then it dissolves into thin air. So there is no nothing to fear.

But if you are intent on hiding some part of yourself – because of a fear that underneath everything you might be an ugly Soul, unforgivable, or deeply evil – then remember this: Evil itself is just an illusion. All evil will eventually dissolve. Love is all there truly is. So once again, there is nothing to fear. The challenge is for you to fall out of love with the illusory image of yourself as dark and evil. No one is. All of you, at your very core, are perfect Children of God. And, as I told you before, you are ALL special.

In light of this, remember that New Age is not evil. Some of my Children are afraid of the idea of New Age. These same Children are often afraid of anything new, anything that is not old and familiar. To be afraid of something new is only fearful judgment.

New Age is simply New Age. When my Children decide to exercise their creativity and move beyond the usual scope of human perception, it is commendable. What is not commendable is to be afraid of change.

Your Father, Christ, and the Holy Spirit ask that you move beyond your limited sense of self and become the Light that you are. New Age is harmless. All power comes from God. People who fear New Age are people who fear dark power. The only real power is the power that comes from God.

If people are into crystals, astrology, tarot, this is usually quite harmless. These things are like grown-up toys. But remember, there is a danger in giving power to something outside yourself. This could mean giving power to something magical. What does this do?

When my Children give away the power that is innate in them as Children of God, they give the protection of their connectedness away. Because you are created as Children of God, you are all, by nature, Children of the Light. You have a connection to the Oneness of the universe. To the Light that God is. There is considerable power in that.

Be aware that there are cults that exist for selfish, fanatical reasons. Beware of being drawn into them. They may distort the Truth. They may victimize their members. Caution should be exercised around any cult. New Age, however, is not a cult.

But still beware. If you decide to shift your God-given power into a belief in something powerful outside yourself – black magic, darkness, evil – then you are making a decision to remove yourself from the natural Light that is a protective force for you. This is risky. In the long run you will move back into the Light. Every one of my Children will eventually. But why remove yourself from Grace and its protection when it is one of your greatest assets?

Perhaps you have a feeling that I do not perceive the type of darkness that you fear on earth. Yes, I live on a plane of Light. I can tell you that fearing others is a paranoid reaction. It leads to separation that will drive your own self into aloneness. Aloneness is not a good place to be. If you have fear, come to me. Come to Christ or the Holy Spirit. Tell us what your fear is. We will give you Grace so that you can appreciate and come to fully accept your own well-being.

People do get lost in the darkness. We were all lost in the darkness eons ago when we chose to separate from God. Why go back there? It has taken tremendous evolution for my Children to reach this far. If you accidentally run into a Soul who is involved with what she believes to be her own personal darkness, rely on Grace to carry you through in your own Light. Remember that people in the darkness hate the Light. If you are in Light, they will be repelled by you.

Remember that darkness and evil are a personal hell and exist only in separation. You have nothing to fear. Those Souls who live in separation are not in union and camaraderie with their fellow man. They do not see themselves as part of the Sonship or as part of the Mystical Body of Christ, as some call it. Pray for the day when your brothers and sisters will let go of their lost-ness and rejoin each other totally in unity and oneness.

Many of the people in the New Age process are trying to practice some of the newer concepts that I am sharing with you.

Your responsibility in this life is to grow and to expand. The New Thought movement has been in progress now for over one hundred years. It is the human potential movement and it is where you should all be headed. Many of the Souls active in the New Thought movement are simply learning new ways of thinking and acting as Children of God.

You all must evolve from your old habits of "safeness" and "comfort" and respond as true Children of God. With confidence you will learn to exercise your freedom as a Soul and leave your safe, comfortable recliners where you observe the world through a glass tube (your television). This is not living. This is an illusion of living. The danger is that you can become stuck in passivity, as an observer of life. And what is worse – you could die in that limited frame of mind.

Some of you may criticize me for asking you to grow. My Son, Jesus Christ, asked people to grow and the world of His time attacked Him for it. New ideas are often attacked by Souls who are in the safety of the mainline. Be careful not to adapt to this defensive attitude. The ego hates to change.

Change is hardest of all for conservative people. When you are asked to become a Light, do not fear the ridicule or the responsibility of the mission. The Light of Christ will shine from within. You will not make a fool of yourself. Other people in the Light will be able to see the fire of Love within you. You will be safe.

Do not exercise fear around new thoughts. Limited thinking is not spectral. As a Child of God, you are meant to be multi-faceted. Be open to the

Light. Be open to exploration. My Grace will protect you from wandering off the path.

In closing, do not fear New Age or New Thought people. They are your brothers and sisters. They are listening for the Truth, too. They are trying to open up to the Holy Spirit within.

DRUG ABUSE

In your recent human era, certain drugs and their usage have brought much pain and suffering to both children and parents. It has been a major problem of this last century. I am speaking both of herbal drugs which are referred to as recreational, as well as chemical derivatives, invented by man, that distort the minds of my perfect Children of God.

Many of my Children (including my adult Children) are pulled toward the use of drugs because of a desire to escape from responsibility. Many are looking for a place of comfort and Peace where they can withdraw. Yet others may be looking for a thrill – primarily at the outset of their drug quest. And once the initial thrill of the drug is over, many Souls keep trying to return to the same old space of drug comfort.

Why does this happen? It happens because very often comfort and Peace are hard for my Children to find in this world. They should be found through spiritual discipline. But instead, these Children seek to achieve that state of mind quickly through chemical means.

Many of my Children find comfort in the world because they know that I, Mary, or Christ, or the Holy Spirit are here to bring great Joy to your heart. But some Souls have not yet arrived in that position of understanding. They cannot feel this Peace, so they try to achieve it artificially through drugs.

Drugs tire people out. There is a wastedness that comes from drugs. It is sacrificing the whole mind spectrum of Light and Love for a tiny slice of that spectrum that is intense and distorted. Some of my Children do this because they are bored and they want an adventure. But there is a price to pay for this adventure. A clear mind can also be a fabulous experience, but of course you have to love yourself.

There is a great sadness in trying to find Peace of mind through the use of drugs and chemicals. The Soul is actually searching for a kind of Heaven that it remembers – a Heaven that is comforting, exciting, complete. It is seeking a place where the Soul feels exhilarated, powerful, beautiful and all-knowing. This is the state to which they want to return, even if they are not consciously aware of it. And some of my Children addicted to drugs are willing to punish themselves temporarily to get there. But they are looking for an artificial "heaven" or "rush" or "high." The experience is not authentic when it is chemically induced.

My Children lost on drugs are often very sensitive Souls who feel the pressures and heaviness of the world. And so they seek escape. But an artificial escape does not last long enough to be comforting. And, of course, there are costs relating to this experience, so the experience is doubly expensive. The drug process robs the mind of its equilibrium. It borrows from the body and mind energy. And this torments the Soul even more – because it is trying to reach a Heaven that it cannot achieve at this point in time. That is what gives the drug user such a sense of wastedness. Drug users often know they are reaching for an illusion – and their egos will keep trying to move into the illusion to find Truth, which of course is elusive under drugs. It simply reconfirms the old rule of the ego: *Seek but do not find.*

And what can you say to such a Soul that is hurt and crying? Sometimes to a Soul on drugs there IS nothing to say. The pain is so deep that only a hug will do. Or a long, loving look that will reach to the Soul.

Yet there would not be so much drug use if the world were a gentler, more joyous place to live. Your economic system can create considerable pressures on people. The further down the economic chain, the more trying it can be. But whatever the circumstance, drugs are never the answer.

I am here to offer you a solution. The only solution that will work is Love.

Love can work in a myriad of ways. Love can heal the hidden corners of the mind, the hidden corners of the heart. Love can transform a mind exhausted by drugs. Both Love and a gentler world can keep my Children from running head on into this most mean and difficult of illusions.

IMMIGRANTS

One thing I want to mention – something that I feel a nurturing Love for is the cause of immigrants. Are there any among you whose forefathers were not immigrants *at some point in time*? I think not.

All of you who have comfort and security now are descendants of former immigrants. You and your ancestors have had the Grace, the benefits, and the advantages from your country to become "comfortable," to become "insiders."

Are you not willing to share? Are you fearful of scarcity and lack? Do you not see that it is your brother, the Christ, who is the immigrant? Whatever you deny Him, you deny yourself.

Do you not see that in a few years you, too, will be an immigrant at the gates of death? And do you not ask for a gentle, hospitable welcome on the other side? Do you not see that you will be an immigrant to Heaven some day?

Then do not see some of your brothers as outsiders. See them as insiders. See them as you would see Christ Himself. Welcome them with genuine Love. Upon your death – this is how you will be welcomed to Heaven – in a spirit of acceptance and genuine Love.

As my Son told you, "Do unto others as you would have them do unto you."

Part Nine

Sacredness

SOMETHING THAT NEEDS MORE EMPHASIS IN TODAY'S WORLD IS sacredness. Television has made people more skeptical and, as we said before, cynical. It has given many of my Children a false sophistication. But it seldom has given them the gift of sacredness.

Churches sometimes offer the gift of sacredness to my Children in their services. But often churches cannot provide the deep sense of sacredness that my Children are looking for. Many of my Children have a deep sense of mysticism. They are looking for a place of deep Peace and reverence. That type of sacredness is hard to achieve in a church service that is a very "busy" experience. By this I am speaking of a religious service where there is an overabundance of prayers and hymns and rituals. When there is constant busyness in your church services, could it be because you are afraid of slowing down — slowing down and hearing?

Most of you need more sacred time to quietly commune with your Heavenly Father, with me, with Jesus Christ, and with the Holy Spirit. I encourage you to create services of deep spirituality and sacredness that are built more around silence and an appreciation of Love's presence. Fewer words, more inspiration.

Many of my Children long for a church with services that have a grandeur and quietude with which they can resonate. As a result, many people have found their sacredness in nature, or in themselves. Or in quietude, in music, in art, in solitude.

We would do our Children a great service to bring more sacredness into their lives, and that is one of the things I intend to discuss in more detail in a later communication with you.

Life itself is sacred. Souls are sacred. Sacredness is a value – a sensitivity of the Soul. It needs to be more a part of your lives. Relationships and friendships used to be sacred. Sacredness brings loyalty, great Peace and fulfillment.

Sacredness is a way of honoring oneself, inside. Sacredness on the outside mirrors the Divine inner realm of sacredness. It wakes us up to the Divine within.

Rituals make us sensitive to that sacredness within. Sacredness brings us more formality, more discipline, and more respect. Not just for others but for Self. Sacredness brings us closer to the deep inner yearning for reunion with God the Father.

Sacredness brings us the Peace that is often missing in our lives. The Soul hungers for sacredness. It longs for the union it remembers with something far greater than itself. Sacredness is at the core of its memory. When you live in a busy, fast world of doing and accomplishments, there can be an empty feeling that follows. The Soul needs to replenish and rebalance itself by being in a Divine space of sacredness. The Soul needs quiet and space to maintain its grandeur. Nature can help. The Soul needs silence to re-balance.

If it doesn't receive restoration from time to time, the Soul can become exhausted. That is why Sundays are needed for restoration. Some quietness, solitude, a chance to be alone and just BE are very important.

The Soul is naturally gentle, playful, and light. The heaviness of this world steals from the Soul's basic nature. My Children, allow yourselves the time to BE. Enjoy your Self for the wonderful diversity you have. Respect your need for space. Time. Quiet. Solitude. These are the things the Soul needs to maintain its balance in the busyness of the world.

Apologize to no one for the time you need to be alone to keep your Soul nourished. Do not always give in to the demands of others, especially when they impinge on your sacred time. Try to sit quietly some time of each day without doing anything. Just be. It may bother others to the point of distraction, because it is generally accepted in the world that you are supposed to be DOING something all the time, except when you are staring into the TV or sleeping. Know that you are permitted to simply BE, and I highly encourage you to sit quietly, with a personal sense of solitude, in Peace.

In a later message to you, I will examine the art of sacredness. In it, I will relate to you the importance of Grace, Discernment, Joy and Laughter to achieve your Heaven on Earth.

WHY STRUGGLE THROUGH LIFE?

Life is a struggle – only if you see it as a struggle. Many people around you may not be struggling at all. There are young people who have not yet begun to struggle. There are older people who have grown tired of the struggle and have given it up. And there are those in their prime who decided never to struggle.

Remember that you are not involved in the *struggle* of life, but in the *process* of life. Many experiences will occur during your human lifetime. How you choose to react to them is entirely up to you and your own Free Will.

Why choose to struggle? Is struggle not similar to playing the victim? Did not Jesus tell you to look at the lilies of the field because they neither toil nor spin? Did he not say that even Solomon in all his glory was never arrayed like one of those lilies?

Choose to live by Grace. Grace allows you to live your life in process, with dignity and Joy. Struggle is concurrent with Fear. Remember, always, that you have a choice. Choose to live your Divine inheritance of Grace. Grace is concurrent with Love. Grace is a choice – an educated and loving choice.

GUILT

Guilt is an old part of your thought process. Guilt is the old portion of your mind that still believes in the devil and hell and punishment. If you aren't good enough – if you haven't atoned for your sins – you may ultimately be punished. This is your ego talking to you.

The world has been run by fear for many centuries – for many millenniums. Fear has always been used to manipulate and to control people. There are still some religions that teach by the "fire and brimstone" method. Fortunately, most of religion by fear has died off.

Look at my Catholic Church. It teaches and lives a gospel of Love. It was not always this way. But today the Catholic Church has relaxed many of its controlling rituals, and it is more modeled after my Son's teachings of forgiveness and Love than it was a century ago. As a result, the Church has expanded and grown and is stronger than ever across the world.

Guilt is the veil between you and God. It holds you back from enjoying His presence. It tells you that you are not good enough to be One with your Father. And thus it keeps you from direct contact with Him so that you cannot hear His words of Love.

Guilt is such an enormous aspect of the Undoing. Guilt is where we will have much work to do in my forthcoming book. I will help you peel the layers of guilt that have kept you earthbound for so long. It is an important part of your process to become wholly free.

HAPPINESS

My Children, happiness is the state of mind of Heaven, and yes, you can achieve it on earth. There are a number of ways that you can open up your heart to experience happiness – and I will share them with you. They are part of the Undoing.

As you undergo the Undoing on earth, the old opposites will not make as much difference to you as they did in the past – right and wrong, black and white, good and bad. They are all about distinctions. They are what happened to the human mind in the Garden of Eden. It is what happened to Adam and Eve after eating of the tree of the knowledge of good and evil. That caused duality in thinking. Good and bad. Your Father does not think that way. Christ is not limited by good and bad, and you will not be limited by duality when you complete your path with the Holy Spirit.

Being "right" is an addiction that can keep you from happiness. Being "right" keeps you from being a truly free person. Think back to the idea: "Nothing is either right or wrong. Thinking makes it so."

So I ask you, would you rather be right? Or would you rather be happy? This is the whole world of dualistic thinking. It is impossible to achieve true, lasting Peace or happiness with this way of thinking.

And so you may say: *"I want to be right and happy!"* And this may seem like the perfect answer for you, but that is not the point. When you can cease to care about being *right* all the time, *then you may have the gift of true happiness.* That is how it works. You have to give up this divisive point of view to achieve the integration of happiness.

There is great limitation in right and wrong thinking. That is because it is all intricately tied up with judgments. Whenever you judge anything in the world, you are judging yourself. And so you are stuck.

So I ask you, would you rather be right…or happy? Choose happy!

To choose to be right means having to defend yourself and an entire complex world of choices. It can lead to madness if you take it intensely and seriously.

Choosing to let go of the addiction to be right is an important new step toward becoming truly happy. You will gain the gift of happiness by letting go of your need to be right. Choosing happiness is the simpler, freer choice.

To choose to be happy is to choose simplicity. And once you begin making choices in favor of simplicity, you become more like your Father. To be God-like is not to become more complex, but to gain the strength of unity and oneness that comes from integration and simplicity.

Choosing to be happy is the first step toward achieving freedom in the Sonship. It will give you freedom from having to be right all the time.

GRATITUDE

Another element of happiness is gratitude. You cannot be truly happy unless you are grateful for who you are – a Child of God – and grateful for who your Father is – and grateful for all the many blessings of this life. This is a key element.

Your gratitude should extend to who you are, and to your mate, your children, your family, your home, your job, your community, and your very life. No matter how great or how simple, how commonplace or extraordinary, gratefulness comes from seeing through the eyes of Love.

Gratitude should spill out of your heart. The more you think about gratitude, the more you will find to be grateful for. Gratitude will be like a fountain in the center of your being. And everything that happens to you will cycle through the fountainhead of gratitude. And this will fill your heart with a quiet Joy or an exuberant Joy, but Joy in either case.

WONDER

Another element of happiness is wonder. Wonder is the reverence for all living things, from the smallest pebble to the highest mountaintop. Wonder is an appreciation of the mystery that the consciousness of God created your life, and all the life that you find all around you…from a newborn baby to an angel, from a tiny wildflower to a mighty tree, from a tiny ladybug to a great white polar bear.

When there is a sense of WONDER…When it is tied in with GRATITUDE just for having been created…When this is coupled with FREEDOM – freedom in the Soul to choose to be happy and to not care about being right – when you have these THREE QUALITIES present, then you have HAPPINESS.

Happiness is your natural state of being. Once you have Happiness you are free to create the *Happy Dream*. This means that once you have accomplished the Undoing, once you have taken your life apart, consciously, then you are free to re-create it with Love. And that is the Happy Dream. It is a milestone in anyone's existence, for when you reach that level, you are free to create Heaven on Earth.

When my Son Jesus explained that we need to become like a Child to enter the Kingdom of Heaven, this is what He meant. For when you have achieved the freedom to choose to be happy, and when you have consciously cultivated the awareness of gratitude – gratitude for Who you Are, and What God Is – then when you integrate this with the Wonder of God and all existence – then you are in the Happy Dream, consciously created with Love. Remember this and work toward it all your life, for it is one of the great milestones toward being reunited totally in Heaven.

YOU ARE SAFE

It is wise for you to come to realize that you are safe. There is a beautiful future ahead of you. Death is nothing to fear. Your only job is to learn to live Love. Every time you choose Love you are choosing me, you are choosing Christ, you are choosing the Holy Spirit, you are choosing God the Father. Eventually we will all be One again. You have nothing to fear.

This is an important part of my introductory message to you. This message is for every Child, every Woman and for every Man in the universe. Please read my books – or if reading is not easy for you, listen to my tapes. You will receive a totally new grounding in life over a relatively short period of time.

I am here to be truly helpful to you. I will ground you in Love. I will help you to forgive. I will help you remember how to be HAPPY. I will open up your life in many new, exciting ways. As your Blessed Mother, I am here to nurture you and to extend the Love of our Father.

Part Ten

Being A Big Person

MY CHILDREN, I DO NOT WANT YOU TO BE CONTENT WITH littleness, with being resigned to a life of quiet suffering. That is NOT the point of life. The age of martyrdom as a virtue is over. The idea of suffering as a virtue is also through. God does not give us suffering to challenge us. We give suffering to ourselves.

Suffering makes us ineffective. The point of life is outreach and inter-cooperation, not the isolation that suffering often brings.

You were NOT placed here on earth to live out your life in quiet submission or suffering. This is a very important concept to grasp.

You ARE here on earth to live a life that reflects the magnificence of God. Just as there is grandeur in His Being, so should there be grandeur in yours.

Both men and women are meant to live BIG lives – living Love in a grand way. This comes from a certain attitude and means living without fear. The thoughts I would hold up for you are big-heartedness. Expansiveness. Touching the lives of others in a big way.

WAKE UP FROM DREAMS OF LITTLENESS!

My Son, Jesus Christ, has sent me to you with a Message. And I say it with a big letter M because it is an IMPORTANT Message:

Wake up from your dreams of littleness. I am here to remind you of all you are and all you can be.

It is your patterning to live out the grandeur of your Father. When you think of grandeur think of generousness, wonderful possibilities, service to others, sharing, exciting visions and fun.

BEING A BIG PERSON – GENEROUS AND GIVING

Do not be afraid of bigness, for it is in your nature as a Child of God.

If you have perceived me as a shy, quiet virgin, resigned to a life of sorrow because of my Son's crucifixion, please think again.

I have a magnificent mission – a great one. I touch the lives of hundreds of millions of my Children each day. I have taken on the responsibilities and the joys of nurturing all my Children throughout the world and the universe. I am there for each one of you who calls on me.

This type of Light-giving is its own reward. I feel the grandeur of Our Father within me. I feel the magnificence of the Children of God. And so I am here to tell you this: *There is no limit to your Soul.*

Look for men and women in the world who live by greatness. You will find them. They are in your neighborhoods. They are on the media. They are in your schools. They are in business. They are in the home. There are men and women who truly live the grandeur of their Father. Focus on them. Make them your role models.

Some of them live this way because of the power of what they do. But you do not need a position of power to live your life in greatness. I want each of you to live out your lives with greatness, not because of WHAT you might be in the world, but because of WHO YOU ARE as a Child of God.

My Son sent me to say that we must have a speedup, a Celestial Speedup. At the current rate we will not achieve the Second Coming for a long, long time. While it is true that there is steady progress on earth, it is going too slowly. The media sends out confused and fearful messages that often cause humans to react with doubt and fear. We need more Light from our media. We need our world leadership to be educated in the ways of Light so that Light will penetrate and spread worldwide.

My Son's message is that Souls on earth must shift from living out dreams of littleness to living out their Light with dreams of greatness.

BEWARE OF LITTLENESS

The world often settles for littleness, with the idea that littleness can bring contentedness. But littleness will never content you, and it will only delay your homecoming. People settle on littleness out of fear or from not being encouraged to expand their vision. People can also fall into littleness unless they have leaders who show them what bigness is.

The only thing that will content you is magnitude – a bigness of Soul – because that is your true nature. It may be hard for you to make the shift, but it will be a tribute to you as a Soul. Think of it as one of the major missions of your life.

You do not have to strive for magnitude because it is your second nature. It will flow from you easily. It will give you a great sense of ease and expansiveness. Others may not appreciate your magnitude because it may threaten them. But seek out your greatness. Develop it. Use it. Live it. And in doing so, you will be kept safe in my Grace.

You will have to be vigilant about relapsing into littleness. The world of littleness will offer you many tempting little gifts. Self-pity. Self-sacrifice. Martyrdom. Indecision. Victimhood. Helplessness. Personal hurts. Excuses.

Resentments. But do not fall in that direction. I am asking you to shift into the greatness of all you are. I am asking you to BE greatness instead of confining yourself to littleness.

This means to become responsible for your own life. This is a big decision to make. But the Holy Spirit within will help you to make this shift, as will I.

Please remember that littleness is hard to leave behind. While littleness is small and shabby, it is one of the traps that is "familiar." I am here to inspire you to move beyond your dreams of drab familiarity to dreams of greatness.

Help one another in this process. Form a small group of three to ten people. Know one another. Support one another. Meet to support your greatness. It may feel unusual at first, but as the energy grows you will know what I am speaking of. I will discuss my Mary Evenings a little later on. And through them you can work on your greatness, encouraging one another to be great Children of God. And it matters not what you do. The form is not as important as is the intention. With strong intent, whatever you do can be done with greatness.

This friendship/support group will help you to help one another to grow into magnitude. I assure you there will be many teachers who will be brought forth to help you understand the idea of greatness and to grow to that level. I will help organize such groups for you to help you grow into greatness.

Once this world begins to live from a bigness of heart, you cannot imagine how wonderful the energy will be!

You will dissolve your old ties to guilt and weakness and you will find yourself standing in an aura of grandeur that was really there all the time. Like all miracles, your initial discovery of the magnitude and expansiveness within you will be a very quiet and moving experience. But it has the power to quake the universe with the thunder of its silence. Be grateful that the time has come for this shift.

LOVE AND FEAR

My Children, we are coming to the end of my message. So let us simplify. And let us do this very briefly. There are really only two emotions – Love and fear.

All of the positive emotions flow under Love: Joy, Happiness, Peace, Gratitude, Laughter, Forgiveness, Outreach. Are you feeling happy? Love is at the root. Are you feeling peaceful and joyous? Love is at the root.

All of the negative emotions flow under Fear: Hate, Anger, Guilt, Depression, Sadness, Jealousy, Envy. Are you feeling depressed? Fear is at the root. Are you feeling sad or angry? Fear is at the root.

So, if you do not like the emotion you are experiencing, you have the power to choose again. You never have to be stuck. You are not a victim.

The point of life is for you to choose Love. Choose Love in everything you do. Do the right thing for the right reason: for Love. Do this and your heart will always be joyous!

You have the power to choose Love whenever you want. I am here to help my Children learn the benefits of choosing Love, of being Self-directed. That is the only way to be strong enough to bring Light and Love to the world.

The old way of seeing things spiritually was to be passive...

Show me what to do...

Lead the way...

I am not worthy...

In truth, there is so much chatter in the world, so much noise and busyness, that many of my Children could not hear the response to "show me what to do..." So in many cases they did nothing.

That is why I am here as an envoy of Christ, to carefully delineate a new way of seeing Love and creating Love in your hearts. When we begin to talk about willfulness, which my Children need in order to make the right decisions in this world, we must also talk about balance.

As you begin to make choices for Love, those choices will need to be discerning. You each have your Higher Self and your ego self. Let us call the ego your "world self."

Your ego is the little voice that will remind you to pay the bills, to save money, to watch out for problems. But always remember that it is very fear-oriented. Let it be your reminder for the important practicalities in life. Pay the bills. Solve the little daily problems. But do not let your ego become the guiding force of your life!

You will need to achieve a balance here. The Higher Self always needs to be in control. Your ego-self will not "go away" just because you have decided to achieve a higher spiritual consciousness. The ego still has some important contributions to make in life. But the ego must never control your life, because it is the voice of fear. The ego makes an excellent servant, but a terrible master.

Keep your ego under control as you would keep a small child disciplined. Thank the ego for all the ways it is helpful to you, but do not live by all of the limiting, fearful thoughts the ego may want to impose upon you.

Your Higher Self can show you how to be happy, how to have fun. You can live in the world, but not be owned by the world. Your Higher Self will have an allegiance to a higher voice within, the all-knowing Self. It will also show you the way to God, to Heaven, and to freedom. The important attribute of the voice of your Higher Self is that it is based on a loving and disciplined presence of mind.

SPIRITUAL DISCIPLINE

Please understand that there is an important element of spiritual discipline that you need to cultivate in your life. Without spiritual mind discipline, your life will be at the mercy of the winds of change. You will have no control as to your moods, your learning experiences, or your life-path. I am here to help show you how to achieve this inner spiritual discipline that will help you achieve a Heaven on earth.

This does not mean that you must stay "happy" one hundred percent of the time. Love has a great vocabulary of emotions that you may choose for variety. You might be in the mood for Excitement. Adventure. Wonder. Laughter. Joy. Exhilaration. Peace.

With spiritual discipline based on Love, your life can take off in an unlimited number of fascinating ways. This is something you must learn to do, not only for yourself, but for you to teach to your Children, your grandchildren, your parents, your grandparents. As a Child of God each of you is a born teacher. I will introduce you to a new way of seeing so that you will have something new of GREAT value to share with others.

A DIVINE SHIFT FROM ORDINARY LIVES – MY PERMISSION

To those of you who are leading quiet, ordinary lives, I say relax and be at Peace. If you feel regret because your life is ordinary, then there may be a missing factor. It may not be the ordinariness of your existence but the lack of inner connection with the Divine – with God's communal energy – that is missing. If you decide to re-establish this connection, you can take the most ordinary life, or job, or relationship, and change it dimensionally into an experience of wonder.

A quality life is not necessarily a matter of quantity – how much or how many. It is often a matter of quality – how deep, how full, how connected.

The most ordinary life can become the most extraordinary life with a shift in consciousness – what we call a miracle. It is a new way of seeing.

If you have the will, the intent, to connect yourself with your Divine Inner Child – that is enough to accomplish the shift. It is a very quiet, a very subtle thing.

I am now giving you the permission to make this shift – to connect with your Divinity within. With trust in me and desire on your part, we can accomplish this together. And when we do, you need never suffer from the ordinariness of life again. You will be re-connected to wonder and to an inner joyfulness that you forgot you had.

It will take spiritual discipline and a new, fresh way of thinking to accomplish this. But if you follow me in this process you will see your life getting better and better each day. This next chapter has some Truths that should help you to grow into the Light.

Part Eleven

Living Your Life With Spiritual Intelligence

MY CHILDREN, I WOULD LIKE TO MAXIMIZE THE TRUTHS OF WHAT I HAVE have been sharing with you in this message. I am doing this chapter for your benefit to clarify, simplify and summarize some my messages in this book. You may feel free to copy this chapter and share it with your friends. Please tell them that it came from me and that it is my gift to them. Here is my summation:

MAXIMIZE YOUR INHERITANCE

LIVE BY GRACE. Because you are a Child of God, you have an enormous inheritance you may not be aware of – Grace. Grace means that you have a natural protection system at your disposal. It is available to you if you are not living in fear. With Grace you are safe – even if you walk through darkness on your path through life.

SHINE YOUR LIGHT.

The other wonderful part of your inheritance is that you really ARE a Child of God and you are connected to God and His Divinity. Your destiny is to rejoin Him. Your inherited Light comes from within and no one can put it out or take it away from you. Keep your Light burning brightly. It is your passion, your Joy of being, of living, of loving.

REMEMBER: THERE IS NOTHING TO FEAR

THERE IS NO THOUGHT OF A PUNISHING GOD BECAUSE GOD IS LOVE. Your destiny is to return to Him. Forget about ideas you might have had about hell. In the long run everyone will be rejoined, and "saved," to use the older Christian concept. Re-enlightened is more in line with the actual process of what will happen.

BE ASSURED THAT YOU ARE FREE

YOU ARE NOT A VICTIM OF THE WORLD. You have Free Will and are responsible for your life. It may take a shift in consciousness to realize this fully. The only thing that keeps you hostage is yourself and your fears. Dissolve them by seeing anew — through the eyes of Love.

HAVE FUN

CHOOSE TO BE HAPPY. Remember that seriousness gets in you in trouble. Forget about trying to be right all the time. Happy is where you want to be. Seriousness is *not* a virtue. Laughter is closer to Godliness. Cultivate laughter, fun and jokes in your life. Share this with others to maximize enjoyment in life.

MAINTAIN YOUR HEALTH, SPIRITUALLY

YOU ARE NOT A BODY. YOUR BODY IS HERE TO SERVE YOU. Do not let it lead the way. You have the authority to keep your body in control and make it behave however you want. Remember also, that health is a gift that you give yourself – a decision you make consciously. You control what goes into your body and how it is maintained. You can give yourself permission to have good health – if you love yourself.

CHOOSE LOVE IN EVERY INSTANCE

LEARN TO CHOOSE LOVE IN EVERY INSTANCE. All decisions are made either on the basis of Love or fear. Certain lessons in your life will keep repeating again and again until you choose Love as the answer. When you do, those repetitive experiences stop repeating themselves. You will go on to a new lesson of Love. So wake up and stop the pain. Choose Love in every instance.

WHATEVER YOU GIVE IS GIVEN TO YOURSELF

EVERYTHING YOU GIVE IN LIFE IS GIVEN TO YOURSELF. We are all One. Giving in this spirit increases your awareness of the interconnectedness of Souls. Whenever you are being stingy toward others, you are really just being stingy to yourself. The more generous you are with others, the more generous you are with yourself. This has a way of multiplying, accumulating and bringing you good fortune.

KEEP AN OPEN MIND

BE OPEN TO LEARNING NEW WAYS OF SEEING THROUGH THE EYES OF LOVE. This also makes life more exciting and more interesting. It will have a big payoff for you. Be willing to change and let go of the past. Be open to the new. You can only live in the NOW moment. So begin to learn what this means and live it.

LIVE YOUR LIFE TO ITS FULLEST

WAKE UP – YOUR LIFE IS VALUABLE. Reach out. Interact. You can have tremendous growth in this life if you choose. Let my Grace fill you with energy and the flow of Love. See what new, unforeseen, pleasant ways your life may change. Trust in me.

BE COMPASSIONATE WITH YOUR BROTHERS AND SISTERS

OPEN UP YOUR HEART. LET COMPASSION FLOW FOR OTHERS. No matter who they are. No matter what level. No matter whether they are easy to love, or challenging to love. They are on a journey, too. Reach out and offer them a hand.

DECIDE WHAT YOU REALLY WANT IN LIFE

CHOOSE IT CAREFULLY, BECAUSE YOU CAN ACHIEVE IT. Do not be afraid to be specific about what you want in life. But remember that on earth you will always have to pay the price – of energy and time. Also remember not to be greedy or selfish in your planning because you will steal the Joy and fun of it from yourself. If you are living in Grace it will make the accomplishment much easier, because the energy and circumstances will flow beautifully.

LEARN TO LOVE YOURSELF

YOU ARE AN ESTEEMED CHILD OF GOD. Honor yourself. You are a

reflection of God Himself. Make note of who you really are and respect it. Remember, there is only one of you. Treasure your authenticity.

SOMETIMES YOU WILL MAKE MISTAKES

IT'S OK — BRUSH YOURSELF OFF AND GO ON. Whether it was a difficult marriage, a serious illness, a bankruptcy, an accident, put it behind you. Forgive yourself and move on.

FORGIVENESS IS PARAMOUNT TO YOUR DESTINY

YOU WILL STAY STUCK UNTIL YOU BEGIN TO START FORGIVING. The past is over. You cannot improve upon it. You may as well dissolve the past. It is not going to do anything for you. Begin by forgiving the big things in your life. They are the easiest. Eventually you will have to let go of all the little grudges, the ones you love to nurse. The little hurts, the snubs, the people who have cut you to the quick. All must be let go. You are really forgiving yourself. There is no one out there but you. Forgiveness is freeing yourself up.

DEATH IS NOTHING TO FEAR

DEATH IS FEARED BY MANY BECAUSE IT SEEMS SO UNKNOWN. In truth, death is not a great mystery. I would like to share a few things with you, my Children. Because you have Free Will – as a gift from your Father – death is seldom an accident. People usually die when they are ready to die. At your deepest level, you always have a choice in the matter. Yet I should point out that death is not necessarily a choice of which a human being may be *consciously* aware.

Death is simply the changing of levels – from one plane to another. Your death may occur when you have completed all the necessary experiences in this lifetime. Or it may occur when you are mentally so disposed that no new growth is possible in your lifetime. This happens when people become very stuck in their ways of seeing life – and as a result, no new learning progress is possible. Then a type of boredom sets in. Often, Free Will takes over and one gives up the will to live. At that point, the Soul is ready to move on.

Death happens for different people at different stages of their lives. Some live long lives. Others die young – even perhaps in infancy – in which case they may be there only for the learning effect their short life has upon their parents as a maturing experience. But nothing is left to chance.

When God created you with Free Will, in His likeness and image, He meant *Free Will*. He does not end your life against your will. If you are advanced in my way of seeing Truth, you will understand and accept this.

Others who prefer to hold the idea that death is like a thief in the night may do so, but at their own expense. It takes a great deal of personal responsibility to accept that one is not a victim of the world, or of God. We need not be victims. We always have a choice if we wish to use our God-given Free Will.

To those of you who are losing, or who have recently lost, a loved one, please remember this. Everything has a season. There is a time for death that is natural for each person. Let them go with Love. In the process and afterwards, do not choose grief. Choose Love. It is very nurturing to yourself.

Once again I remind you to live your life by Love, and to make all your decisions based on Love. It will give you unlimited Peace once you do this. In this way, you will be able to be very loving to yourself with regard to death.

Part Twelve

My Mary Mission

I am intimate with the Holy Spirit, with Jesus Christ, and with God the Father in order to coordinate my Loving connectedness around the globe. My mission leads me to be available to infinite numbers of Souls across the earth. On the plane from which I communicate, I am privileged to be in touch with billions of my Children.

In order to be in touch with all of you, I have decided to communicate with you through this book, as well as other books in this series in the future. I will write again through this same channel because I have more to share. This way of translating my words clearly, openly and simply for all to appreciate is very much in tune with my wishes.

LOVING MY BOOK

This book should help guide you to a place of Light and more perfect peace. The book has an energy in and of itself. Hold it and feel it and sense the personal sense of safety it brings to you. I want this new book to exhilarate. I want you to sense its Light, its Truth. I want you, my Children, to be imbued with this same Light, with an enthusiasm you may not have felt before in this lifetime. I want you to wake up and start living your lives. I want you to dissolve your depression and begin to thrive on higher forms of energy.

I want to free each and every one of my Children from lethargy. I want to give your Soul a new way of living your life in Grace. I want you to be aware of my Grace surrounding you with all the safety and Joy that comes with it.

You will see more and more of me through this Light in the oncoming years. I will be here consistently to help with your development until we are reunited in a beautiful, boundless integrity that is absolute Oneness. Until that time, my mission is to help accomplish the Second Coming, which is our complete rejoining and returning to our Father.

To those of you who wish to be critical of my Message of Love, kindly remember this. It is easy to criticize. We tried for clarity with every word and sentence of this book. This book is an approximation of the Truth. Before you criticize, I want you to write something with me that is better.

Also, before you criticize me as a modern Mary, I want you to understand the SPIRIT in which my book is written. It is the spirit of Love. It may not appear perfect, but the INTENT is correct. The intent has always been the intent of Love.

To any who wish to judge me, I ask them not to do so until they have completed their lessons of Love. And then they will never judge because they will be beyond judging. People who judge are always judging themselves. And they are always stealing a portion of themselves.

Remember that I do not want your criticism. I want your Love. I want your support. I want your growth. I want your expansiveness, not your littleness. And in thankfulness for supporting me in my quest, I will send you Joy, Happiness and Grace, always.

MARY'S WINDOW IN CLEARWATER, FLORIDA

Have you heard about my window in Clearwater, Florida, the big one on the office building? I am full of Joy and happiness about it. Yes, it is my image on that window. It was a wonderful surprise, an honor to me, a gift of an elderly gentleman in Florida. It is his gift of gratitude to me. He told me we would do it, and I think it is wonderful. He said he would accomplish it as his personal focus, imaging me in my honor. It is one of many little miracles that happen every day. He is a very dear Soul. I have been very complimented, not just for the window, but for all my beautiful friends who have come to visit there in the name of Mary.

A miracle is a natural occurrence and miracles should be happening around you all of the time. To cause an occurrence of my image was not beyond the capabilities of that elderly gentleman. He thought about the gift he wanted to give so much that he first created it in his mind. Then with my help, it became manifest in the world outside.

This is one of your abilities as a Child of God. You do have the power to create – much more than you may think. In time you will learn how to create miracles in your own life, all around you.

MARY EVENINGS

Because spiritual advancement works better and easier when you are allied with a group of loving, like-minded Souls, I am advocating the establishment of Mary Evenings. These are to be evenings of Peace, Joy and quiet learning among friends. They will be safe havens where individuals may learn new spiritual principles in a non-judgmental atmosphere of Love. Participants will have the opportunity to speak the language of Love with one another where they know they are safe.

Speaking the Truth is an important part of your development. When you are able to verbalize the new principles and the Love that is in your heart, you help to create it on a deeper level. Whenever two or more are gathered at a Mary Evening, I will be there with you.

I suggest that someone provide a curriculum for your study at the Mary Evenings. It should be based on this book, and any other books that follow in the next few years. These evenings will not be concerned with religious beliefs, but with spiritual Truths that will help you in your continued growth as Children of God.

My Mary Evenings will be administered through my Mary Foundation. Referring to them as Mary Mornings or Mary Afternoons is also acceptable, but I would like to generally refer to these gatherings as Mary Evenings. Write to my Mary Foundation for information as to how you can form one of my groups.

MARY GARDENS

I ask you to create Mary Gardens in honor of me through my foundation. Each Mary Garden is to be an oasis of beauty, a place of healing and Light where individuals may gather to feel and to enjoy my Grace and presence. My Mary Gardens are to be places of Joy where depression and sadness are dissolved. I want them to be places where happiness wells up in the heart.

I would like their orientation to be spiritual, rather than religious. By that I mean that they are not to resemble a church. They are not to have a group of beliefs that people need ascribe to. They are to be beautiful places where any of my Children may go to feel welcomed, nourished and embraced. They are to be places of freedom and Joy, exempt from authoritative overtones. I would like the first Mary Garden to be built at the location of my foundation. And then I would like other locations to be built, through my foundation, in major cities around the world. Try to support my request in your country so that you can have the benefit of a Mary Garden nearby. I would like them to be comfortable places for all people, including those who have no church or religious beliefs.

In my Mary Gardens I want the level of aesthetics and harmony to be extremely high. I would like my Mary Gardens to overflow with beautiful flowers, gentle music, natural light and a high level of beauty that will reflect and bring forth the natural Joy and happiness in your heart. The purpose of this is to raise your spiritual level higher and higher, so that you will be able to experience greater Joy while on earth.

At my Mary Gardens I want my Children to experience levels of happiness and Joy that are seldom experienced on the earthly plane. In northern climates I would like to see my Mary Gardens enclosed with glass so they will blossom year-round. You can help my Mary Gardens to grow through your support in whatever way you choose. I urge you to take part in my project. I will be there to help with this development each step of the way.

SUPPORT OF MY PROJECTS

As you are probably aware, things on earth happen so much quicker and with much more definition through the simple aspect of money. Money can be thought of as Love in action. It is not that human efforts are unimportant to me in the growth and furthing of my projects – they very important. But I would be extremely grateful for your kindness in contributing money to the growth of my projects. The Mary Centers are for your joy, your growth, and the recognition of your own Light within.

A wonderful way to remember someone you love would be to send a gift in their name, or for their remembrance. Contributions you send me through my foundation will bring you a feeling of Grace, of Peace, and inner Happiness. It will give you confidence knowing you are supporting my loving work. And through our conscious joint intent, the Love Light in all of us will share in our gifts of Grace, Peace, and inner Happiness.

The time is right for my projects to happen in the world. It is time for me to emerge as your voice for Truth and Love and new Creativeness. Thank you for your support of my work. I assure you that your generosity will return to you manyfold because I personally will be indebted to you for your support of me and my work of Love on your earth.

You will see more and more of me in the days and years ahead. You will need my presence for the growth that lies ahead in Love. You will find the coming times to be a very exciting adventure. I will be with you. Stay close to me. Make my work available in foreign translations for my Children through the world. Read my books again and again, even if they seem to be simple to you. Think about them. Talk about them. And listen to my words on tape.

Remember that the only thing that remains of the past is the Love that was expressed: the Love between parents and Children, between husbands and wives, between lovers, between families and friends. That Love is all that remains of the past. All else is gone. Honor the Love. The Love is what He is, what You Are.

The memory of my peace and happiness is to stay with you. I hold you in my Love. I protect you in my Grace. Remember to choose Love a hundred times a day. Each time you do, I am there with you!

The End of Mary's Message

CONTINUING MARY'S REQUESTS

In order to move ahead gracefully with Mary's requests, we have formed The Mary Foundation which will help to administer her wishes with regard to Mary Evenings and Mary Gardens.

We have established a nonprofit corporation to handle the donations that we know will be forthcoming from people like yourself to make Mary's requests a reality. That nonprofit is called Light Education, Inc. and has a 501(c)(3) designation, so that all donations can be tax deductible.

We are open to your participation. If you would like to make a donation toward the Mary Gardens or toward the Mary Evenings or in honor of a loved one, please contact us.

If you would like to help start up a Mary Evening group, please contact us. Or if you would like to inquire about having a Mary Garden in your area, please get in touch with us at the same address below.

If you would like to have a distance healing for yourself or a friend, for any illness or physical limitation, please contact us. The Mary Foundation has an excellent way of accomplishing this. Your participation will help our foundation, as well as yourself, to achieve healing.

Marcia and Allan Schulte, along with Donna Sweeney, will help to guide these projects with a sense of Love, Joy, and underlying Truth. This is for the purpose of doing Mary's work here on earth. Allan, Marcia and Donna welcome your participation and your prayers, and look forward to hearing from you. The website is www.Marysmessage.com.

The Mary Foundation
Light Education, Inc.
P.O. Box 15043
Sarasota, FL 34277

EPILOGUE

MAKING DECISIONS BASED ON LOVE

I am adding this message on to the end of my message because it rounds out my message of Love, and I feel it is very important to the overall process of Love.

When I refer to Love, making decisions based on Love, seeing through the eyes of Love, this is what I mean: Love is always a matter of intent and purity of heart. Please listen carefully, my Children, because this is very important. How you understand and live Love is everything.

One of the main reasons you are living your life here on earth is to learn to make all your decisions based on Love. The purpose of this is so that you can be like your Father in Heaven. He makes all His decisions this way. Since we are made in His image, it is our challenge to get back to being like Him, and this means living our entire life in the flow of Love.

Life is based on a series of decisions. In the process of training yourself to think with Love, you will need to become conscious about those decisions. Living and thinking with love requires a discipline. This is a process that should be learned by children, as well as adults. You should work on the process of Love with alertness. To achieve this you have to be consciously awake, not sleepwalking through life. Eventually, this process will become more and more second nature to you.

Here is how I suggest that you go about the process of making decisions based on Love. There are three parts to this decision-making process. The objective is to do the right thing, for the right reason, and to do it with heart.

The right thing means doing what is right for you on your path through life. What is right for you may be wrong for another. And what is right for you at one time, may be wrong for you at another time. This point requires personal honesty. It is not so much what you do, but the spirit in which you do it.

Many of my Children do the right thing all the time, but they do it for the wrong reason. They do what their parents taught them to do, what their teachers taught them to do, what their church taught them to do . . . perhaps even what their conscience tells them to do. But they do it because they fear what would happen if they didn't do it. Perhaps they do it because they are supposed to — or because they feel obligated to do it — or they do it because of the drudge of responsibility. This does not equate with Love. There are only two choices: Love and Fear. The wrong reason is to do it for fearful or obligatory reasons. That often sets up a quiet resentment, reticence or tiredness that is not part of the Love process.

If it is something that HAS to be done, and done regularly to sustain life, you make the decision to do the same thing, but to do it out of Love. This totally changes the energy for you. Instead of doing it grudgingly, you do it with a flow and an entirely new energy sweeps through you.

My Children, if you can consciously choose to do THE RIGHT THING FOR THE RIGHT REASON - motivated by your personal choice and not obligation - this is in the flow of Love — and it can make all the difference in your life. God gave you personal will power and this is your chance to use it authentically. When you do the right thing for the right reason, you empower yourself, you take on a leadership quality. You have made a decision that transcends being a rule-follower. You are acting out of personal decision rather than obligation. Doing the right thing for the right reason is about freedom. Most important, this makes you feel good about yourself.

So if people do the most extraordinary and complex things, but without Love, they are spinning their wheels. And if people do the simplest things, but with Love in their heart, they are connecting. It is as simple and as powerful as that.

Finally, the third step, you do it with heart. It is very important that along with this decision to do the right thing for the right reason, there must also be an open heart, a willingness. When you consciously decide do something caring for another human being — out of genuine Love, compassion, outreach, empathy — then there is suddenly a heart connection behind the action. It moves you onto an entirely different plane. It connects you with God, with the Christ, and with me, Mary.

When you open your heart - with the right intention - Love happens! You change everyday energy into Love. Things begin to connect - as if by some kind of grace. In actuality it is grace, the actual flow of God-energy that comes from using His Love energy intentionally. When this occurs, your will and God's will are one and the same. This is what I call heart-full. And it will make you feel wonderful! This is how you can bring deep joy and happiness into your lives.

What could be more embracing, more affirming, more enjoyable than honoring God by making the choice to be concurrent with His flow of energy? You are always a reflection of your Father when you decide to do the right thing for the right reason, with heart.

When you reach this level of knowing how to make decisions based on Love, you reach a point where you can see the advantage of always staying completely in God's flow. You then choose to see anything and everything through the eyes of Love. No matter how depressing, how disappointing, how difficult — you can choose to see it through the eyes of Love. When your perception changes and you purposely choose to see through the eyes of Love, that circumstance, that thing, that person no longer has power over you. You can be surrounded by Love if Love is what you decide to see.

This may be a challenge at the start, but once you become proficient with this point of view, you can begin to change your mind to see anyone, anything, everything as part of a Love field. This will have a profound and wonderful effect upon your life.

Once again, I send my Love and will be close with you constantly. — Mary